# The Path ot the Blue Raven

*From Religion to Re-enchantment*

First published by O Books, 2009
O Books is an imprint of John Hunt Publishing Ltd., The Bothy, Deershot Lodge, Park Lane, Ropley,
Hants, SO24 0BE, UK
office1@o-books.net
www.o-books.net

Distribution in:

UK and Europe
Orca Book Services
orders@orcabookservices.co.uk
Tel: 01202 665432 Fax: 01202 666219
Int. code (44)

USA and Canada
NBN
custserv@nbnbooks.com
Tel: 1 800 462 6420 Fax: 1 800 338 4550

Australia and New Zealand
Brumby Books
sales@brumbybooks.com.au
Tel: 61 3 9761 5535 Fax: 61 3 9761 7095

Far East (offices in Singapore, Thailand,
Hong Kong, Taiwan)
Pansing Distribution Pte Ltd
kemal@pansing.com
Tel: 65 6319 9939 Fax: 65 6462 5761

South Africa
Stephan Phillips (pty) Ltd
Email: orders@stephanphillips.com
Tel: 27 21 4489839 Telefax: 27 21 4479879

Text copyright Mark Townsend 2008

Design: Stuart Davies

ISBN: 978 1 84694 238 9

A CIP catalogue record for this book is available
from the British Library.

Printed by Digital Book Print

O Books operates a distinctive and ethical publishing philosophy in
all areas of its business, from its global network of authors to
production and worldwide distribution.

# The Path of
# the Blue Raven

*From Religion to Re-enchantment*

## Mark Townsend

BOOKS

Winchester, UK
Washington, USA

# CONTENTS

# Endorsements

*I LOVED it. I loved the writing and the style. Honestly? I think it is his best yet. There is a lovely, lovely humour in it. I laughed out loud on occasions, and that was one of the things that endeared me to the insights. There are nuggets of pure gold in this book. And Townsend's writing means you don't have to search very hard to find them. A remarkable man with an equally remarkable penetrating insight that is hewn from experience, coupled with the ability to express complex ideas in simple terms. Prepare to look at the world in a whole new light.*
Drew McAdam – 'The Interrogator' from TV's Trisha show

*The Path of the Blue Raven is an extraordinary spiritual journey. It brings to life Jesus' words 'The truth shall set you free'. For Mark Townsend, it is in devastating self-honesty that freedom-giving truth is found. It is this uncompromising honesty that has opened him to the deep flowing currents of mind and spirit. The result is a liberating journey from Christian priesthood, to stage magicianship and the beauty of nature spirituality. It is a journey that is both literally true and profoundly mythic. It is a magical journey. It is a journey that will speak to the hearts of many.*
Revd. Simon Small, Author of From the Bottom of the Pond

*Mark has been bravely transparent in his description of his spiritual journey. We could all do with his refreshing honesty about our own doubts, fears and hopes.......*
Revd. Jonathan Osborne

*Inspirational, and touches chords*
Lorriane Munn - Druid

*You can't imprison the Spirit in a box or a book or a religion for that matter. It finds a way to break free. The Path of The Blue Raven is a pilgrimage to true spiritual wisdom. There is a hidden music in this*

*world and it is there for all to hear and heed. Mark Townsend followed this music and because he did he found keys that unlocked and opened doors of beauty and enchantment. The magic key is love. The magic is with Mark and with this book.*
David Carson – co-creator of Medicine Cards.

*In the history of the Church reformation has come about whenever someone has dared to step out of the official walls and look for truth in the wide world. Mark Townsend does more than step outside the walls of Christian dogma. He leaves behind the conventions that hold back human imagination. In The Path of the Blue Raven he not only shares his own journey, but illuminates the pathway for others whose spirits refuse any longer to be boxed and packaged within the confines of religious organizations. True believers among Christians or Druids are likely to be offended by his words. But wanderers will find inspiration and hope.*
Walter William Melnyk author of The Apple and the Thorn (with Emma Restall Orr) and Marsh Tales and Other Wonders

*I started this book expecting to skim it and found myself reading every page. It is a wonderful quest romance, a story about the nature of religion, magic, England, modernity and many other things as well.*
Professor Ronald E Hutton

*The revolution starts here!*
Phil Rickman

*They slept until the black raven,*
*the blithe hearted*
*proclaimed the joy of heaven*
Beowulf

## Dedication

*To the dear old C of E and the many 'Anglican Angels' I've encountered along the way. No matter how far I travel I will never forget you.*

# Acknowledgements

Many have helped me with this book. Without them it simply could not have been written. Of course my darling wife and children – Jodie, Aisha and Jamie – have had various bits 'tested' on them over the course of the last year. Thank you again for putting up with me and not losing patience. You three mean everything to me!

On top of that 'glorious little trio' there are the many wonderful people who've proof read, offered invaluable criticism, given me ideas, submitted stories and quotes, granted me permission to use extracts from their own books and writings, and supported me in various other ways.

When one submits a manuscript, it begins a long process of copy editing, proof reading and designing. Then there comes a point where its final draft is set and no further changes or additional material can be added. This occurs quite some time before the actual publication date and, in my experience, even after this time one comes across other folk who (with regard to the, as yet, unpublished book) prove to be worth their weight in gold. I'm talking about the critics, reviewers, those who offer endorsements, managers of book shops, fellow O Books authors, members of Writer's Forums, and friends. While I would clearly desire my appreciation of them all to be noted below, it is not possible. I may be a mind-magician but I can't see into the future. All I can do is add this special anticipated thank you to all those who will (in the future) be of invaluable help with regard to the marketing of this book. Your efforts and advice is always truly appreciated.

Now, with regard to those gemstones I can name, the following have been put in alphabetical order:

Pauline Kennedy Allan, Jeff Ball, Alistair Bate, Maria Beaven, Cherie Blair, Heather Blakey, Sébastien Beaudoin, Paul Brook,

David Carson, Rob Chapman, Damh the Bard, Danielle, Mike Danata, Judy Dinnen, Rob Draper, The Druid Network, Gill Edwards, Wendy Ellyatt, Enrique Enriquez, Barbara Erskine, Tim Freke, Uri Geller, Caroline George, John-Michael Greer, Álvaro Herrera, Julia Heywood, Heike Killet, John Hunt, Ronald E Hutton, RoMa Johnson, Hans C Kamerman, Marcus Katz, Kenton Knepper, Sarah Kral, June-Elleni Laine, Kim Lloyd, Matthew Long, Marion, Drew McAdam, Walter William Melnyk, Ragen Mendenhall, Thomas Moore, Lorraine Munn, Robert E. Neale, Adele Nozedar, Lin Oberlin, The Order of Bards, Ovates and Druids, Jonathan Osborne, Peter Owen Jones, Anthony Peake, Jinny Peberday, Gerry Proctor, Rhonda Rawlins, Lizabeth Rider, Richard Rohr, Romany, Mark Rosher, Bella Rowe, Gerard Senehi, Simon Small, Jenny Smedley, Ray Thompson, Tess Ward, Madeleine Walker, Gary WhiteDeer.

I also with to thank the following authors for their inspiration as well as the permission to quote from their own books: Eugene Burger, Philip Carr-Gomm, Trevor Dennis, Tom Harpur, Thomas Moore, Bob Neale, Emma Restall Orr, Simon Parke.

On top of all these marvellous writers there is one other person who has graced this book with the most powerful of Forewords. I am speaking of the amazing bestselling novelist, Phil Rickman. Thank you so very much. I am indebted!

And finally the Blue Raven herself. For your guidance, inspiration and for teaching me that I too have wings... *thank you!*

# Foreword

## by Phil Rickman

I'm not sure exactly when the Church of England began to lose the Mystery, but the process has certainly been accelerating of late, and if this is one reason why the biggest Sunday congregations are now in DIY superstores, who can disapprove? Who can say there isn't more spiritual fulfillment in repainting the kitchen and fitting a new cat-flap than mouthing trite hymns to a background of beeps from the pew behind, where bored kids are playing electronic games on their mobiles? If you haven't been exposed to one lately, this is what the Church calls a 'family service.' Most people claim to feel better when they come out because... well, at least they got through it without too many conspicuous yawns, and the guitarist wasn't bad.

Of course, there *was* a time when a church would be a strange, numinous, glowing place, and going inside would be about entering a different level of consciousness. And when you emerged you'd feel different because you *were* different. It wasn't so much about piety and dogma as experience, sensation, transportation - a reminder, through actual awareness, of *something else.* Some people do still get that feeling, but they're more likely to be the ones who converge on Stonehenge, pre-dawn, at midsummer - the Church having dumped the magic.

Ten years ago, I began what would turn out to be a series of crime novels, seen from the point of view of an Anglican priest - a woman - who was appointed diocesan exorcist. The idea was that it would examine human evil on a different but still realistic level, but I knew that many readers wouldn't relate to what I thought of as a mainstream vicar. I needed a maverick, someone openminded, someone flawed, with human failings. So Merrily Watkins is a single mother with a cigarette habit. Her least-favourite word is 'pious', and if she drops a plate, she mutters *shit*, rather than *Oh bother!* Oh, and her teenage daughter has pagan inclinations with which Merrily occasionally feels some kind of half-guilty sympathy. Expecting the clergy to be outraged, I waited for condemnation from a thousand pulpits. It didn't come. Yes, there *has* been outrage - but it almost invariably emanates from 'traditional' churchgoers rather than priests. Priests have, in fact, been unexpectedly supportive. Slowly, I discovered that Merrily, with her doubts and questions, her experiments with meditation, her feelings of spiritual loss and her suspicions about the Church hierarchy, was far closer to the norm than I could have imagined.

And I've become aware, too, that within the Anglican Church are the stirrings of a new rebellion. There's almost a parallel now between priests and police officers who can't get on with the job because of too many rules, too much protocol, paperwork and political correctness. There's a yearning to rediscover - and share - something closer to the roots of spiritual experience, closer to the Mystery. When Merrily's daughter, Jane, suggested that maybe nobody should be allowed into a church service between Baptism and the age of sixteen, I began to think that maybe the kid was actually on to something.

It's become clear that the political rows about gay clergy and women bishops are concealing something far more profound, while the Church has been doing its best to quench the spirit of priests like Mark Townsend.

Read on. The revolution starts here...

# Prologue

## The Blue Raven Goddess

There was once a Celtic Island far out to sea, whose main inhabitants were beautiful black ravens. Apart from the worms, bugs and washed up fish, on which they survived, these majestic birds were the only creatures. They had all the usual raven features – jet black eyes, black beaks and bodies to match, deep frog-like croaks and an altogether eerie elegance. Yet there was something different about this tribe – they could not fly. It seemed that somewhere back in the mists of time these great wolf-birds had lost the ability to travel through the air. They still had wings, but just saw them as a nuisance.

One day there was a ferocious storm and the birds huddled together in their ground nests. All day and night the rain poured down and the wind blew hard, ripping up trees and throwing branches across the land.

The next day, when the sun rose and peace returned to the isle, one of the more adventurous young ravens decided to walk to the far side of the island to inspect the damage. The isle was battered, and the broken branches that littered every inch of the ground made walking very hard for this young bird. But there was one place that seemed uneffected by the storm. He could see it in the far distance - the great (and forbidden) hill known as Raven Mount. It stood out above the level ground and had a huge ancient tree on the very top, which was still standing. The young bird decided that he must climb the hill and find out why the tree had not been torn up like all the others. It was a long and difficult climb, and on finally reaching the summit he curled up beneath the great tree, exhausted, falling into a deep sleep.

He dreamed of how that very tree was once a home for his ancestors. He dreamed that, somewhere far back in time, ravens

3

could build nests in trees...

It was the sound that woke him! There, above his head, high up in the sky was a black dot. And the dot seemed to be making a noise – a noise that sounded familiar. He rubbed his eyes and saw that the dot was now bigger, and it was coming towards him. Suddenly he realized what it was – a bird like him, yet different, blue in colour, and... swimming through the air! He realized at once that it was a goddess, and he bowed low to honour her arrival.

The blue raven landed and said, in the sweetest voice, 'Brother, don't fear me, and don't bow down before me, for I am no different to you.'

Lifting his head the young raven saw that this flying bird was indeed just like him.

'But you were swimming through the air and you were blue like a goddess', he said.

'I am just like you.'

'But why are you here?' said the young one.

'I was traveling, high in the sky, when a great storm blew me off course,' she answered, 'I then noticed your island so I flew down to rest before I find my way back to my own'.

'So,' said the young one, 'can I swim in the air like you?'

'Yes,' she said, as she jumped into the sky stretching out her broad wings to demonstrate. Once again she started to turn blue as the sun-filled sky and the deep blue waters reflected and glistened on her oily black feathers.

'You *are* a goddess,' he shouted.

'Only in so much as you are a god my little brother,' she called back.

An hour later, and after only a few bruises, the young raven was also flying so, together, they flew back to the other side of the island.

Meanwhile the rest of the tribe were busy tidying, when one of them looked up and noticed the two blue-black birds in the air.

Opening his own wings and studying them with increduality he said to himself, 'So that's what they're for'.

Soon, most of the birds started making their way to the forbidden hill, where they would climb up and jump into the sky... and as they did, so each one turned into the colour of the gods.

Back on the ground, however, remained the few tradition-alists who much preferred the safety of the ground, 'This is all ridiculous,' they muttered, 'It'll all end in tears.'

Looking down and seeing their expressions the blue-raven goddess smiled and, offering a silent wish on their behalf, left to find her own home. It was a day the tribe will never forget. The day when they uncovered a gift they'd had in their possession for decades, yet could not see.

Mark Townsend

# Introduction

Ravens glisten in our dreams. For millennia, they have inspired the Native American, Asian, Norse and Celtic worlds. The raven, whose black coat shimmers with a translucent blueness in the sun, is a powerful symbol of transformation. To many cultures, the raven symbolizes initiation into a magical path. Like the infamous and oft-misunderstood death card of the tarot deck, the raven speaks of leaving one stage of life's journey to discover another – a fresh opening through which earlier struggles, now understood, become the pathway toward spiritual gold.

This is a perfect picture of my current situation, for it has been a painful coming to terms with all the mess of the past and a gradual uncovering of what I call our 'inner gold' – the magic of the true self. I am beginning to develop a sense of the magic that flows through every molecule of our awesome planet. My blue raven is a mythic soul-friend who beckons me forward to face new challenges, open myself to life's mysteries and trust that I too can fly. And because she symbolizes my journey so powerfully I have not only used two raven myths (for the Prologue and Epilogue), but have also selected some of my favourite raven quotes and passages to head all the chapters of Part Two – *Into The Realm of the Ravens*.

Thus the book you now hold is the story of a struggling man who all his life has wrestled with questions, searched for meaning and discovered it in unexpected places. It has no ulterior motive to convert, influence or argue an opinion; nor will it claim any particular religious path, philosophy or theory to be the 'ultimate truth'. It is simply an attempt to be honest, human and realistic about what we might call the quest for enchantment. As Thomas More says, 'The soul has an absolute, unforgiving need for regular excursions into enchantment. It requires them like the body needs food and the mind needs thought.'[1]

*I feel that need.* Every day I experience a magnetic pull towards wonder and mystery. For many years I thought I could satisfy my desire by immersing myself within a religious organisation. Those years were special. I learned many things, but I did not find the long lasting, soul enriching enchantment I longed for.

I started to uncover the reasons for my dissatisfaction as I wrote my first book, *The Gospel of Falling Down*. Writing often brings with it the therapeutic experience of self-teaching. It is as if the very act of opening ourselves to our deepest thoughts unlocks a voice within that is not often adequately listened to. That book taught me many lessons. One of them is that we stand on hidden treasure, and only prolong its discovery by searching for it elsewhere. I was struggling within a religious world that seemed to place the object of our quest somewhere 'out there.' It saw the spiritual life as a constant climbing of a ladder towards a 'God' who was placed out of reach. The task was to struggle, strain and strive to get close to the reward, the 'treasure' of salvation. However life has taught me that the greatest treasure is often found when we collapse from our egotistical efforts to climb and achieve, into a broken heap at the bottom of the ladder, where our cracked shell exposes the hidden gold at last – our divine-self. I can now understand why the rigid and burdensome world of organised religion never really freed me. It was a barrier to the divine rather than a doorway.

I'm not alone. Many people are in a similar situation - a place of deep openness towards spiritual things, yet profound disenchantment with formal, mainstream religion. The religion I come from is a Christian tradition. Indeed I served as a Priest for ten years. I still find the person of Jesus intensely exciting. His stories continue to send shivers down my spine. I have not tired of the Church's founder, but I am tired of *Church*ianity. In this book I will seek out what for many in that tradition have been forbidden fruits, exploring the rich terrain of the more native, druidic and earth-based spiritualities.

As well as being an ordained Priest I am a magician (conjurer). Magic has been a happy companion of mine throughout these years of disillusionment. I have performed, semi-professionally, for over ten years and my performances have changed dramatically over that period. My magical journey is a necessary part of this story because it has brought the deepest insights into how to live an enchanted life. Stage magic (the art of illusion) keeps alive the possibility of real magic. In such a rationalistic, left-brain western world, magic has fanned the flames of my more intuitive and imaginative faculties. And within a perfection driven, success orientated and often literalistic modern Church culture, magic has been a powerful symbol of the more mysterious and mythic dimensions to faith.

So this book represents the beginning of a new adventure in my life. It is the closure of one door and the opening of another. The door of disillusionment that I close is the world of institutional religion. The door of re-enchantment that I step through is the world of non-dogmatic spirituality. It is a strange feeling. I am in two states at once – both extreme disillusionment and profound re-enchantment! It is a journey that is taking place as I write, and I want to describe much of it as it happens. It is divided into three parts:

Part One, *Disenchantment*, tells the story of my long-term love-hate relationship with the Church. A word of warning! It is (out of necessity) rather irreverent in places. It's the way I cope when thinking about past experiences, some of which would have crushed me completely were I not to find the humour within them. In any case when I laugh, my loudest cries are always directed at me and the ridiculous situations I got myself into. Learning to laugh at oneself is one of life's greatest forms of liberation! Not laughter as ridicule, but laughter as a gentle acknowledgement of how what seemed so serious is all really very trivial.

Part Two, *Into the Realm of the Ravens*, describes how a 'chance' encounter with a spiritual tradition vastly different to my own, triggered a new phase in my journey - an opening up to deeper enchantment. Being a nature-based path this experience has helped me to understand and tie together the many quasi-druidic experiences I've had over previous years. The process of re-enchantment is occurring as I write and, because I want the book to be totally authentic, I will describe some of it as it happens.

Part Three, *Tales from Beyond the Magic Doorway*, is a beautiful collection of real-life accounts of others who've stepped through a similar 'magic doorway' into the re-enchanted world of nature-based spirituality. Among their company are an International Bestselling Novelist, a Christian Bishop, a French Canadian Potter, an American Indian Artist and a US Navy Sailor (who was once a Catholic Monk!). I invited them to share their unique stories because I am utterly convinced they will ring loud bells and offer much comfort to like-minded seekers.

If you are, or have been, part of a traditional faith and feel you are missing something, or if you are seeking the magic of the divine within, then this book is for you! In sharing my journey, and the stories of others, you will be introduced to a world of like-minded people - ordinary people who have stepped off the mainstream, onto the path of personal magic. I invite you to walk with me as I tread this well-worn path. And who knows? Perhaps together we shall be enchanted, inspired and brought close again to the magic that dances under our feet.

# Part 1
## 'Disenchantment'

*Many people define their religion as a belief, and they pin their hopes and understanding on a provisional understanding of life. But there isn't much room for faith in a religion that is reduced to belief, and there isn't any place for an open-minded appreciation for the world's sacredness. In a disenchanted world, for all its concern for morals and social action, religion separates itself from everyday life and becomes obsessed with its own brand of belief and moral purity. In this kind of setting, the people who pollute our rivers and oceans and exploit workers and families may go to church and profess strong moral values, and yet they don't have any conscience about the water, the earth, or the human community.*

*There is something dreadfully wrong with this kind of religion, which creates a kind of psychotic dissociation. A person feels morally pure because he is blissfully adhering to ideas of morality that have little to do with the world in which he lives, and at the same time he is committing heinous sins that are not catalogued in his disenchanted morality.* **The source of our modern discontent is the loss of natural religion...** (my emphasis)
Thomas Moore[2]

# Chapter 1

# Pawns, Squirrels and Jesus Freaks

*Can you see into the future?*
*And picture your tomorrow?*
*Can you send your soul on a riverboat*
*And look ahead for sorrow?*

*And if you could see pain there*
*Around the riverbend?*
*Would that not halt your traveling,*
*And all adventures end?*

*So rather, live today*
*And don't anticipate!*
*Take a risk, trust the hunch,*
*The river will not wait.* [3]

A year ago, if I'd have known what *was* around the river bend, would I still have triggered a course of events that were to lead to one of the most desperate years of my entire life? Would I put myself, my darling wife, my children and our families through all that again, just for the sake of making what most of my friends saw as 'a reckless decision'? The answer is an unequivocal 'yes'.

In June 2007 I resigned from ten year's ministry as an Anglican[4] priest because I was haunted by the heaviness of past mistakes and needed to rid myself of their power over my happiness. I found a way to do so that was both honest and private, and which in terms of outcome, could have gone either way. I could have ended up with a clear direction to continue as an official priest of the Church of England, or I could be advised to try a different path for a while. As it happened it was the latter advice I was given – and so my decision saw the evaporation of my vocation, my home, my pension and my financial security, and all this only days after I had returned from a honeymoon.

I will return to this story, for much more needs saying, but first I want to go back *a further ten years* to the time when I first stood in that ancient preaching box – the pulpit.

It was summer 1996, and there I stood in the ornately carved pulpit of the colossal town centre Church, ready for my first attempt to preach as a newly ordained Deacon[5]. I can remember my sermon text. It was not from the bible. I'd opted for something different – very different – the Disney animated film Pocahontas. There is a scene where the beautiful tribal princess is contemplating her future. In typical Disney fashion she sings a song whilst canoeing down a white rapid river, huge waves leaping out at her as she paddles. Her words are powerful and true. They ought to be, for they are based on a saying first expressed by the ancient Greek philosopher, Heraclitus. It's good to know that 2500-year old wisdom eventually finds its way into modern day children's films.

The song's words speak of how much we potentially miss when we decide to settle for a safe, risk-free existence. The context is this: Pocahontas has been betrothed by her father (the chief) to a warrior named Kocuum who is described as 'steady as a beating drum', yet her gut tells her there's more to life, an adventure perhaps. As the song comes to the end the rough white waters settle until she sits in her canoe, floating peacefully on smooth and placid surface. She looks ahead and sees she's arrived at a place where the great river splits into two smaller streams, one of them gentle and wide, the other twisted, narrow and dangerous. As she sits, so she expresses herself through the final few words of the song. Should she take the smoothest course, or does life hold a bigger dream for her?

There I stood, a symbolic six foot above contradiction, in the great medieval pulpit, strengthened by this children's tale. I preached on the notion of Christianity as a risky, dangerous faith - faith that is about facing the deepest questions and not being afraid of the answers; faith that demands spiritual honesty and utter openness; faith that is, in the words of the then assistant bishop, 'a comfort to the disturbed and a disturbance to the comfortable'. I wanted to be a risk taker and a radical, brave enough to speak from the heart no matter what. I willed with passion to follow Pocahontas down that frightening river of rapids and uncertainties. I prayed that I might become a leader who could inspire the bravest faith adventures. I dreamed of being able to be fully myself – warts and all – for I believed in a God and therefore a Church that accepted folk as they were.

Believe me, I tried so damn hard to live up to that inner will, but it was not too long before I found myself paddling down the tranquil and secure waters of, 'better not rock the boat, I've got my pension to think about'.

While I always managed to inject a radical edge into my preaching, the pressure to conform was just too great to be totally myself, especially after I'd moved from my curacy to a second post of Team Vicar.[6] There I slowly began to turn into a clerical pawn on an ecclesiastical chessboard, inferior to all the rooks, knights and bishops. Occasionally I'd seek encouragement from a friendly queen of a different game (the 'chessboard' of psychotherapy). She would give me lessons in tactics as well as help me uncover the skills of my inner knight or the hidden strengths of my under-used king archetype. However, back on my own chessboard, even when I did muster up the energy of the king, I'd only find myself outmaneuvered and presented with a unified shriek of 'checkmate'. I sometimes wished I had the guts to be a real knight and cut them down to size with a metaphorical sword. However something in my psyche, something I have only recently begun to face and overcome, meant that I was often rendered powerless. And so, even in what were apparently placid waters of the quieter stream, I began to drown.

This is perhaps one of the greatest lessons I've learned! What looks like the easier way - the smoother course - is often, in the end, the most life crushing and soul sucking of all, for hidden just beneath the surface of the apparently safe waters, lie fearful creatures that will drain away your emotional strength like psychic parasites! To sell out to such fear robs you of your will and saps you of your energy. Whereas when you are brave enough to face the real world (the rough waters) and be your true self – your flawed and failed and wonderfully imperfect self - you are free in a way that the so-called still waters of conformity make impossible. As Simon Parke says, 'When we feel the need to be seen to be good, like a frightened child, we will pretend in order to please. Pretence kills more people than cancer.'[7]

My spiritual journey began as a late teenager after my stepbrother took me to an eccentric little Pentecostal church.[8] It was all quite magical and had an unashamedly supernatural side. Even that first visit introduced me to the rather odd phenomenon known as speaking in tongues or glossolalia, and after only a few more weeks I encountered full blown 'miracle healings'.

I'd always been interested in magic and the unknown. Even as a young boy I had a magnetic attraction to anything supernatural. When I was about 10 a regular highlight was receiving my copy of Unexplained Magazine which the postman faithfully delivered each month. I'd dash off to read it cover to cover, lapping up all the apparently true stories of UFO sightings, extrasensory perception and ghosts. I was also a student of conjuring after catching the magic bug from my uncle who taught me how to vanish a playing card by sleight of hand. My interest in all things magical (both real and illusionary) is a passion that survives to this day.

Like everything I do, I gave my new-found Pentecostalism

100%. I borrowed books from the library, joined the small fellowship groups and asked a constant flow of questions. Within weeks I knew more about Christianity in general, and Pentecostalism in particular, than many long-term members. After a few more months I'd modified my dress and got rid of any possessions that seemed contradictory to the Pentecostal way of life. I was subconsciously adapting myself to fit into my new spiritual family. In hindsight I can't imagine what I must have looked like to my non-church friends, an 18year old boy wearing a suit and tie, carrying a black leather-bound bible under his arm! To put it in context, only a couple of years earlier I was known for my Bowie-esque orange spiky hair and punky bondage trousers.

Of course no one told me to dress so formally. No one told me I should not mix with non-Christians and avoid pubs and clubs. No one told me to stop smoking or drinking. No one told me to burn my martial arts costumes and awards, my rock LPs or my supernatural books and magazines. No one told me I should start giving 10% of everything I earned to the Church, but I did - all those things. I was becoming a fanatic! I was turning into what some of my work colleagues called a Jesus Freak! I was starting to believe things about God, myself and other people that were completely out of character. It was all part of a honey moon phase as a new convert and I was buzzing with excitement.

After only a year or so I became convinced that I was being called by God to the ordained ministry. Thankfully my pastor was wise enough to suggest a little patience. In the mean time he invited me to do various things within the fellowship, as a kind of in house preparation. He even entrusted me the pulpit! I was about 18 years old and I preached to the whole congregation, for 45 minutes, on the theme of the Adam and Eve's fig leaves! I remember poking fun at both evolutionists and neo-pagans, to the appreciative laughs of the congregation.

Like all honeymoons, I eventually came back down to earth... with a thud! It was my over active mind that did it. For some reason nagging doubts started creeping in. These turned into heavy episodes of analysis and criticism. I can't remember how it all began. I can't remember what the doubts were about, but I can remember the feeling of disappointment when the fellowship's goal posts seemed to change all the time. It was common to hear the preachers talk about a God who would forgive people the most gruesome sins and darkest failures, which is why the church had a constant influx of screwed up, broken and battered new converts. And, sure enough, they'd be accepted and welcomed open armed into the fellowship. Why was it, then, that my mere doubts and questions were seen to be such a crime? Why was I not offered the same grace? It felt deeply unfair.

My questions kept coming, and they needed answering, but the answers no longer satisfied me. Disillusionment crept in as I was given more and more bible text solutions to everything. I remember saying to someone, 'How can we believe the bible is the infallible word of God when it doesn't even claim that for itself? And suppose it did. Wouldn't that only be as good as an accused man standing in the dock saying "I really didn't do it M' Lord, honestly."' There was even a bible text answer to that. It didn't help! The Bible and Jesus were seen as the answer to every question that could possibly be asked, and this I found increasingly nauseating. It reminds me of a joke:

A Sunday school teacher tried a new approach. She said, 'today I have a question for you. What's small, grey, eats acorns and has a long bushy tail?' There was no response, so she repeated the question. Then, after a somewhat uncomfortable pause, an awkward looking boy at the back put up his hand and said, 'well I know the answer must be Jesus, but it sounds like a squirrel to me.'

At that point in my life I worked as a shop assistant in a busy town centre electrical retailers. I was perhaps the worst salesman the store had ever employed. I just found it so damn hard to keep up the bullshit. We were given lessons in high powered sales technique but I really couldn't bare the idea of force-selling items that customers clearly didn't want, need or even come in for. It was a great lesson which I took with me into my life as a clergyman: *don't try to sell people products they clearly don't want or need.*

I'd worked in the store for about three years and it bored me senseless. I had also been having no luck with the opposite sex, as they all ended up trying to control me. So all this, on top of the problems with my church, motivated me to escape for a while. I decided to visit the very country where all this Christianity stuff began... the Holy Land. I thought a long break from life in the UK was well deserved, and perhaps I might find some of the answers I'd been looking for. Perhaps I might feel closer to this Jesus if I visited his home country.

The best way to visit Israel, I soon discovered, was to work on a Kibbutz, and a few months later I was off. I had no idea what I was letting myself in for. The whole adventure is a book in itself and far too much to squeeze into this volume, but what I can say is that I came back totally transformed, though not in the way I'd expected. I went there expecting to be moved and even re-converted by the natural sites of the Galilean lake, the green hills and the Judean deserts. I had imagined that walking on the very ground where those holy feet had trod would be enough to re-enchant my faith, but it wasn't. The landscape was certainly powerful and beautiful but it did not convert me. On the other hand the places I expected to be turned off by - the shrines, temples and holy sites of the more ancient traditions - I found enchanting, mysterious and full of magic (though magic was not a term I would have used back then).

The following extract is from my most recent book which describes my experience in one such holy place, The Church of the Nativity. It is the great basilica built on the traditional site of the Magi's visit to the infant Jesus in Bethlehem:

It was the 7th of December 1988, the run up to Christmas and, if one time of year has ever given me goose bumps of enchanted anticipation, Christmas is it. I guess it all fits in with my love of magic. Since early childhood I've experienced Christmas as a thoroughly spellbinding time of year. The dark nights and colored lights, the brass bands and Carols playing in shops and arcades, the frosty weather and Santas on sleighs, I love it all. Each ingredient adds to the atmosphere of excitement and wonder. I believe we *need* a sense of wonder, mystery and enchantment in our often over-serious 'grown up' lives. We need to have the flickering flame of our long forgotten childlike imaginations rekindled so we don't lose touch with our inner child. Of course this inner child is wonderfully far less immune to the contagion of Jesus than the rational adult of our normal personas. My experience that Christmas, as I sat in the belly of Bethlehem's great Temple to Jesus, was one such experience of divine contagion.

I had tried three times to get to Bethlehem. It was the anniversary of the intifada, so things were more than a little difficult, and my two previous attempts at catching a bus from Jerusalem to the 'little town' were obstructed by strikes. However, my third attempt was a success. The short journey took me past the little hamlet of Bethany and out into the Judean hills. As far as I recall the whole trip only took around half an hour – perhaps even less. I got off the bus and stepped into a market square. There were armed soldiers everywhere but the Church was right there. I entered the tiny little door in the front of the ancient building and entered the huge basilica. After a little search I found another doorway and a passageway with steps down to some sort of crypt. It was clearly the way to something special for there was a constant flow of people coming out from the passage.

I climbed down the stone staircase and found myself entering a magical world not unlike the Christmas Grotto set up in an old English mining cave that I visited with my wife and children last Christmas, though there was a tangible difference to *this* 'Christmas grotto'. Of course, it should not need saying that at the heart of the Christmas story is not a fantasy or a magical fable but a real story about a real human family who, like all of us, had to face real human concerns. It is a story of physical exhaustion, homelessness and human birth in the most unprepared and altogether unhygienic of labour wards. But there I sat, on a ledge inside the Holy cave, and watched as pilgrim after pilgrim brought their gifts to lie at the symbolic place of Jesus' birth. Some brought candles, others brought coins, and still others lay on the floor and kissed the gold star marking out the divine birth place. It was like watching the Magi bringing their gifts. From every corner of God's green earth they came. It was pure enchantment. I remember thinking about the first Christmas and wondering what the actual Magi had been like. I also wondered about the parents of Jesus and then the infant himself. What an awesome image this is... this first picture of the saviour's birth. It is an image so powerful because it is about God plunging himself into our messy, confusing, painful and thoroughly human lives, our thoroughly imperfect human lives.[9]

It was a moment of enchantment even if the sacred site did contradict my Pentecostal sensibilities. The grotto was over the top, glitzy and steeped in traditions that I had no time for, yet it moved me to the point of tears. I even knelt down and kissed the floor where a gold star marked the divine-child's birth. Not for a minute did I believe it was literally the place of Jesus' birth, but that didn't matter. I joined in the ritual and came away with a precious gift - the gift of re-enchantment, a gift that opened closed windows inside me, and let in a gust of air that dislodged a few of the more hard line assumptions and views I'd picked up along the way. These folk knew something about deity! These folk, whom I would normally have written off as superstitious, were in touch with a deep spirituality – and that was astonishing!

Visiting that land also changed my perspective. It was a broken country of inter-religious struggle and warfare. Back then I didn't know enough about the situation to make any judgments, but the pain and misery on both sides of the divide was impossible to avoid. I began to wonder how, from this context of heart-felt daily prayer for the peace of Jerusalem, I would ever be able to settle back into a religious world that now seemed so trivial by comparison. Not a few times in the past had I offered up prayers to 'Almighty God' for a parking space!

On my return to the UK there was no way I could slip back into Pentecostalism. For all its emphasis on the supernatural experience of God I now found it rather predictable and dull. Its preoccupation with church services, church prayer meetings and church house groups now seemed far too inward looking. I found its heavy emphasis on 'unwavering faith' and 'biblical authority' now far too controlling and closed. Four months earlier I'd left England expecting to return having been injected with a new dose of religious zeal, convinced of the reliability of the Bible and the uniqueness of Christianity etc. Instead I came back even less convinced about those things but with a hunger for mystery and enchantment that needed satisfying... *I was on a quest!*

Chapter 2

# Pistols, Python & Hateful Epistles

*The trouble with so much of civil religion and cultural Christianity*
*is the lack of this religious experience. Such people tend to get*
*extremely rigid, dogmatic, and controlling about religion. It's*
*almost as if there is an anxiety in them because they know they*
*haven't really experienced it yet. Missing the sense of the whole*
*they cling to some small part.*
Fr. Richard Rohr[10]

My quest eventually led me to the Church of England. I
remember it happening - the eureka moment! I was sat in a place
where my friends and I used to play - a big green park called The
Quarry. I'd been busy trying to work out what I was going to do
with my life now I'd come home. It was confusing because, while
I knew I couldn't continue as a Pentecostal, I still carried a
distinct sense of vocation. I needed to find a faith community
where I could express my spirituality as well as explore the possibility of ordained ministry; but it needed to be a place that could
cope with my open mind on the one hand, and my passion for
mystery and enchantment on the other.

Then I noticed it, jutting out above the roof tops and trees, the
stubby point of a church's spire. It was the very church where the
tediously dry and totally compulsory school communion services
were suffered by a teenage Mark Townsend and his rebellious
friends. It was also the very church where, quite a few years
previously, I'd managed to sneak in and find the record player
that played phoney church bells music at God-only-knows how
many decibels. I never did find out whether they ever actually
played the Sex Pistols LP I'd left on the turntable. The

mischievous part of me still enjoys the thought that one particular Sunday morning, a few decades ago, the poor unsuspecting verger unwittingly treated his quiet middle class neighbourhood to a mega-watt helping of *'I am an Antichrist!'*

Catching a glimpse of that spire sparked a thought... *be a vicar!* The Anglican Church was not something I was wildly attracted to but, having attended two C of E schools, I knew enough about it to suspect it might be just the place for me. I knew of its liberal side because I used to take the pee out of it for that very reason, 'Ha ha, those Anglicans! They all believe we came from apes etc.' (yes I was once a 'Creationist'). Likewise I was aware of its evangelical wing because my step-brother occasionally took me to a very successful Anglican evangelical youth group. This was comforting because I was still quite suspicious of those who would 'water down scripture to nothing more than mythology' [oh how I had *that one* completely the wrong way round]. On top of all this I was also conscious that, though it could not compare with the mystical havens of the Holy Land, the C of E had a deep sense of connectedness to the past and an unashamed use of symbolism in worship. So I decided to go and talk it through with my ex-secondary school head of house, a chain-smoking Anglo-Catholic called Fr. Geoffrey Burgeon. He'd always been a caring teacher, especially during the period of my parents' divorce. I thought he might be able to point me in the right direction. So I rang and arranged a visit.

After two hours of excellent conversation and non-stop passive smoking I came away with a chest-full of Rothmans and a meeting arranged with the Diocesan Director of Ordinands (DDO). Fr. Burgeon had informed me that it might take anything up to nine years to become a vicar. First I'd have to choose a church to attend regularly. Then I'd need to make myself busy by taking on various minor liturgical roles, such as putting out hymn books and reading the lessons. Of course I'd have to get confirmed too. I'd then need the eventual sponsorship of the vicar to put me forward to the DDO who would assess my vocation and possibly arrange a meeting with the Bishop's Examiners. If all that went well the bishop himself would want to see me and, if he approved, I'd be sent to a selection conference for three days grilling. On top of all that, as a lad who'd completely screwed up school, I'd also need to educate myself to the level of someone beginning a course at a University [i.e. five O levels and two A levels]. Not much to ask! Amazingly, at some point in the conversation Fr. Burgeon decided he'd by-pass the first bunch of hurdles and ring the DDO then and there, and to my surprise the voice on the other end of the line agreed to see me.

Walter the DDO was a remarkable man; tall, introverted and spiritual. I thoroughly enjoyed my meetings with him and the little exercises he set me. Within a year I'd jumped most hurdles and become an official ordinand. Due to being 'the new boy on the Anglican block' and having a very slender academic background, I was required to do two years non-residential training on the excellent (now defunct) Aston Training Scheme, followed by three years residential college training.

Aston was an amazing experience. It was an intense course of spiritual exploration, theological reflection and academic preparation. And, because the intake came from a huge variety of church traditions, it was a real melting pot. There were Anglo-Catholics who were so high church they made the Pope look like a protestant; evangelical-charismatics who made my Pentecostal days seem about as joyful as a Plymouth Brethren prayer meeting; and liberal-radicals who believed in... well, to be perfectly honest I have no idea what. Then there were all shades in between. I loved it and recognized, over those two years, a gradual 'sliding up the candle' (moving towards a catholic spirituality) as well as a growing appreciation of the liberal tradition. I was falling in love with the powerful, almost magical, use of rich symbolism in worship (which was inevitable when you consider how moved I'd been by my experience of the 'smells and bells' customs of The Holy Land). I was also enjoying the freedom to make my own way within all the muddle and mess of Anglicanism. The only criticism I have about all this variety and diversity is that I found within each sub-group the same kind of narrowness and *'we're the true way'* that I had encountered in the church I'd left. I can never cope with this mentality, whatever tradition expresses it. Within such groups I usually end up playing devil's advocate. The greatest commandment was never 'always be right' but 'live in love.'

By and large Aston was a soul-enriching time of opening up to each and every experience that was on offer. I lapped it up. I also began to detect something in myself – along with my growing catholic heart came a deep insight that the body (and all its senses) can be used in ritual and worship. I built myself an altar at home and decorated it with icons, statues, religious artefacts, flowers, rocks and stones. I made a prayer stool and would happily kneel there for hours in a blissful haze of incense smoke and candle light.

I had a particular fascination with icons,[11] one of my very favourite being Our Lady of Vladimir. It is a breathtakingly beautiful depiction of the Blessed Virgin Mary holding the Holy Child. For some reason the images of Mary were almost more endearing to me than the little Christ figures they clutched. Another that I still find awe inspiring is the 'Our Lady and Child' statue in All Saints Church, Hereford. I used to leave candles burning in front of her as often as I could. I now recognise this growing appreciation for Mary's place in my devotional life as a deep stirring in my soul for an expression of the divine-feminine.

To safe guard against 'Mary-olatry', Anglicans (and Eastern Orthodox Christians) insist that these Mother and Child images are not statues of Mary but of The Incarnation – the being born as human of God. Therefore they should never depict Mary alone. I always appreciated that safe guard and can remember getting all confused over the Church's mixed views about Mary. Even though I loved her images I always had a problem with the more elaborate Marian doctrines, for they seemed to separate her from us. To me she was a simple young woman who happened to say 'yes' to the divine. She was like every other soul who has lived and, rather than being exalted high above common humanity, is a symbol of what's true for the whole human family – we can all be 'God-bearers.'

Looking back I now see Mary's images up there on pedestals as testament to the deep inner spiritual need we have for a Mother Goddess. In a religion that has been dominated for centuries by belief in a *Father* God, who incarnates as a *male* Christ, who chooses 12 *male* apostles, and whose church is run by a *male* priesthood, the natural divine-feminine longing cannot be quenched forever.

Thinking about my catholic tendencies reminds me of one of the many angels I've been blessed to know - Fr. Austin Masters, my Aston-designated personal Tutor. Fr. Austin was a wise Anglo-Catholic monk, and Canon[12] of Hereford Cathedral. He'd been a well-respected advisor on all things ministerial for decades. I found him delightful, and we remained friends long after his duties as my tutor had come to an end. I adored exploring all my theological and ecclesiological[13] questions with him, and he simply loved being able to be there as a sounding board. My first ever sacramental confession was with Fr. Austin and, though I shouldn't say this, it was a scream. At that point in my life I thought I was drinking rather a lot. I'd been teetotal throughout my Pentecostal years, so a large gin was, to me, 'a large sin'. I confessed my dreadful alcoholism to Fr. Austin. He allowed a little silence, and then gently asked, 'Exactly how much *do* you drink Mark?' I told him. 'Oh that's just dirtying the glass M' boy,' he said, 'Get on with you!' The man was a star!

Whenever I receive negative or nasty mail, I often counter-balance the effect by remembering the deeply affirming letter Fr.

Austin wrote for my end of training report. He said: 'In all my many years of meeting and helping ordinands, I have never met someone in whom I so whole-heartedly approve'.

After Aston came three year's theological training at a prestigious theological college near Oxford. One of its nick names was 'The Bishop Making Factory' and, though there would never be any chance of that for me [I'm far too uneducated, worldly, scatter-brained *and heretical*] my name would one day be officially put forward to Downing Street as a nomination for a Bishop's post by my local MP and great guy, Bill Wiggin.

By the time I started my college course I was also married and the father of a simply adorable little girl.[14] The college was extremely academic and 'blessed' with a severe case of intellectual snobbery. On my first visit I came across the names of the prospective students on a notice-board. They had academic titles alongside them so we knew exactly who had what degree, doctorate etc. Since I was one of the minority with nothing I thought it would be fun to write my *highest* qualification alongside my name. It ended up saying *Mark Townsend - O Level Art.* I sometimes think I would have been far more suited to the first theological college I considered. Funnily enough it was closed down shortly after my visit! What I most remember about it was the Eucharist[15] I attended. Some of the very high church students had designed the service and were referring to it as 'the marse'. They'd been a little over-zealous with the thurible[16] and, consequently, created enough incense to smoke a batch of haddock. Then, out of the clouds, came this dancing mad man, who was apparently supposed to be taking the collection. He bobbed up and down the aisles shoving an offering plate in front of people's noses shouting, in a Palin-esque accent, 'Spare a talent for a poor ex-leper'. I ended up in a far more serious place.

In the end I came away with an Oxford honours degree in Theology at a grade that was more than satisfactory. But college was not just where I gained academic skills. During my final year

I decided to find myself a totally non-religious hobby so I wouldn't end up overly absorbed by Churchiness. I re-kindled my childhood interest in magic and, by the time I was 'let loose' on a congregation, had become a member of the Hereford Magical Society and the International Brotherhood of Magicians. Another year or two and I'd also be a member of the prestigious Magic Circle.

As a brand new clergyman I was still under the illusion [excuse the pun] that this was just a hobby - a necessary antidote to all the Church stuff. How wrong I was. Within weeks I discovered I could make good use of it in a ministerial context! I began performing magic within school assemblies and family services, and it worked! The rather shy new deacon had found a way of making his children's talks both alive and memorable. It wasn't long before people started referring to me as 'the conjuring curate.' Then folk began inviting me to functions for adults as well as children. Soon the local and regional press got interested. I even had a few TV appearances. But the attention was not all positive. After one particular headline in the local press I received this anonymous letter:

A <u>True</u> Christian resident of…

Dear Rev. Mark Townsend,

I was <u>disgusted</u> to read in the Journal of your devious method of attracting people to church. Obviously you do <u>not</u> read your Bible, or you would plainly see that such practices as magic, sorcery, witchcraft, divination and the like, are <u>absolutely condemned</u> in God's Word (e.g. Deuteronomy CH 18: 9-12)

I just cannot believe <u>how</u> such a person as yourself came to be an <u>ordained priest</u>. I mean, did your authorities know of your practises? <u>If not</u>, small wonder the church today is in dire straits, and this is <u>just one</u> of the practices accepted by the church nowadays.

Magic and sorcery belong to <u>the darkness</u> of this world, and we all know who is behind it. God's Word is <u>the light</u> and the right way to go. HIS SPIRIT IS <u>NOT</u> IN DARKNESS, OR WITH IT. (John 3:19-21). I'm sure I speak for many.

Since then I've had a steady flow of similar correspondence, though some of it is expressed in a more loving tone (even if it does, in the end, consign me to the flames!) One letter once called me 'a rudder on a ship that leads people to hell'. My mischievous side wonders whether I should use it on my website as an endorsement! Or how about a stage name: Mark Townsend – Rudder on a Ship to Hell!

Another time I received one that complained of my 'magical practices' and then invited me to look up Deuteronomy 18 v 10 - 12 [can I really be bothered?]. It concluded by kindly expressing, 'How dreadful it must be to be known as someone who is detestable to the Lord.'

What actually amazes me is not that these people hold the views they do, or even that they feel it's appropriate to send such incredible letters, but that they are comfortable themselves with such a 'God'. Their God views me, and all other magicians, as 'detestable!' I'm afraid I feel my brain beginning to leak out of my ears when I try to understand how a 'loving God' can 'detest' people.

I've shown this letter to friends, 'But why don't you just write back and point out that your magic isn't real?' they say. The answer to that is simple; even if it was *real magic,* I would still feel as confused by such a view of 'God', and I do not want or need the 'blessing' of folk who's opinion of *real magicians* is so low. Over the last few years I've had the privilege of becoming the friend of many who come from magical nature based paths (Druidic, Wiccan, Shamanic, Native American, New Age and Eastern). I wonder how they feel when they hear such cruel things being said in the name of 'God'?

So I keep my collection of hateful epistles as a reminder of what religion can do to otherwise sensible and loving people.

# Chapter 3

# The Three Magics -1

*It would be easy to dismiss deceptive magic as empty and meaningless, but deception is too functional a human behaviour for this type of magic to be completely condemned. Fooling and being fooled are common experiences in everyday life. Deceptive magic has the potential to entertain and educate us with this troublesome experience. Theatrical deception reminds us that we can be fooled, that everything is not necessarily as it seems - a reminder that can be both fun and functional.*
Robert E.Neale[17]

When I look back over the last ten years and consider how my magic has developed I can detect three distinct stages. Each of them marks not just a magical development but also a new phase within my spiritual journey.

During my time as a Curate I explored how magic could work as a tool for communication, but I was concerned about how it might be viewed. My cautiousness was prompted not just because of the hate mail, but because I knew that magic tricks depend on deception, leaving me with the question, 'is it morally acceptable to use a deceptive art form within a religious context?' I therefore needed to think very carefully about how to present my magic and how to answer any questions thrown at me. An example of the kind of objections I receive can be seen in the following letter to the local press:

'To use deception as a window to God is highly dubious. I have always believed that, at the very least, using his magic tricks in a Christian context, Mark should be prepared in the end to show how they are done, after all they are playing on people's naivety, and those people are worth more than that.'[18]

In other words I should only do magic tricks in a church if I then show that they are not real magic by exposing the method. However I suspect that most audiences (even Church ones) are already well aware that they are tricks, and I imagine they would feel cheated rather than valued by their new insight into the previously secret mechanics. No, if magic is performed at all then it must be performed competently and without exposure. But that does mean the use of deception. So how do I answer the objections?

In fact I found it easier to answer than I'd expected. You see the vast majority of people (even members of the most conservative churches) practise 'deceptive magic' themselves, they just don't realise it. For example how many parents have ever crept upstairs on Christmas Eve and delicately filled their little darlings' coloured stockings with nuts, satsumas, a cracker and a few other goodies? What parent is not filled with joy as they watch their enchanted little-ones ripping open the gift boxes they believe came from a magic-man with a white beard, who entered their house via the chimney, dropped off his gifts and then flew away on a sleigh pulled by reindeer?

*That's not deceptive magic!* I can hear your thoughts. But I'm afraid it is. A magic trick is precisely what it says; a clever use of *tricking (deceiving)* people into thinking that magic has taken place. Magic tricks use misdirection, sleight of hand, clever wording, stories and a dose of play-acting to create the *illusion* of real magic. Some magicians call themselves 'actors playing the part of magicians'. Make no mistake, for the young child on Christmas morning *real magic* has taken place. Gifts have appeared that were magically brought from the North Pole via a special reindeer delivery service. And who was it that caused this magic to occur? Well the children think it was Father Christmas but the grown ups know who it really was. *They* were the magicians who, behind the scene, created the magic that enchanted their children. They used storytelling (the tale of the Father Christmas myth), misdirection (the waiting until the child is asleep), sleight of hand (carefully removing the stocking and filling it with gifts), and a touch of play-acting (some folk even dress up as Santa in case a child is not fully asleep).

Those who've played the Tooth Fairy and actually lifted up the child's pillow while she slept to switch a tooth for a coin, are perhaps even more qualified to call themselves magicians. Again, for the child, real magic has happened. A fairy came in and magically turned their tooth into a coin. What could be more magical than that? Yet what both these scenarios require (for the magic to work) is deception – the harmless white-lie of creating fantasy by play-acting. Very rarely do parents ever suffer heavy guilt-pangs when they talk about Father Christmas as if he were real. I believe he is real, not in a literal sense of course but in a mythological sense, and we keep that magical myth real and alive by telling the story and making the magic. Therefore my argument is that the vast majority of people – conservative Christians included – do sometimes unwittingly act as magicians to their children.

Of course there are a tiny minority who choose not to entertain *any* notion of Father Christmas (or the equivalent) because they feel it is a harmful lie which distorts the true meaning of Christmas. Some even refer to him as *Satan* Claus. A few years ago I heard about a Christian Minister who accepted invitations to visit primary schools over the pre-Christmas period, but abused his position by telling all the kids the 'truth' about Santa. He let them in on the secret (exposed the method) and told them it was not a man in red but a mum or dad who left the presents. In so doing this Grinch in a dog collar stole these children's Christmases. He robbed them of a precious gift that we usually lose at a much older age – the gift of enchantment.

So you can see that, generally speaking, the deception objection is quite easy to answer. Most people, once they recognise their own willingness to play along with the magic of Christmas, drop their loaded guns to the ground. The minority, who see all such fantasy as lying, and therefore evil, cannot be argued with, and it really isn't worth the energy anyway.

However there is a second objection, a more sinister one, which must be taken very seriously. It comes from the incredible joint-assumption that 1) *he really is* doing magic up there on the stage and 2) magic is against scripture and therefore he must be of the devil. The amusing thing is that it is usually only ever adults who actually think I'm doing real magic when I make a severed piece of rope join together again, or cause a coin to vanish under a red silk. After a show most children dash up to me saying, 'Can you teach me how to do that?' or 'Where can I buy that magic trick'. Unlike the myth of Father Christmas and The Tooth Fairy, most young kids have sussed that magicians are play actors who use illusion. They also know that they could do it too, should they be able to acquire the necessary knowledge and props. In contrast the minority of adults who object on the 'satanic' grounds actually do believe that I can make coins melt away into thin air or float six foot above ground. If I could, would I really be living in an ex-council semi and driving a battered old Peugeot estate?

I was particularly amazed by one letter I received. To be fair it was warm and genuinely had my best interests at heart, but it was also full of heavy assumptions. Incredibly, it was from a 'Christian Magician.' He spoke of how he used his own magic in schools and youth groups. However, even he (as someone in the know), expressed his concern for the state of my soul. He'd seen a picture of me 'levitating' my son (a cool trick called the Chair Suspension). However, rather than taking the time to phone a few magic dealers and find out that he could have bought the necessary kit to achieve my little publicity miracle for about £250, he sadly concluded that my 'skill' was demonic in origin.

Again, there's no way of arguing with such opinions if that's what folk choose to believe. If people really insist that David Copperfield can actually fly over his audience or walk through the Great Wall of China by real (demonic) magic, then I'm not going to be able to convince them otherwise. With regard to my own shows the best I can do is use a disclaimer. I often used to say something like this: 'I'm going to show you some amazing magic, but I want you to know that all of you could do what I'm about to do if you learned the tricks. It's not real magic you see. It's what we call illusion'. And when performing within the context of an actual church service I'd use my magic primarily as an illustrative tool. I'd say to the congregation, 'I am going to show you an illusion that will illustrate what we've just read in the bible. As an art form it's just like using any other skill as an object lesson – like painting or dancing.'

This was the first stage of my magical development. I was so conscious of how folk could potentially misinterpret my magic that I covered myself to an extreme, and thus saw my conjuring as nothing more than an elaborate audio-visual tool. The second stage occurred some years later… during my next post!

# Chapter 4

# Holy Sh*t!

*'I gathered all my courage, as though I were about to leap forthwith into hell-fire, and let the thought come. I saw before me the cathedral, the blue sky. God sits on His golden throne, high above the world – and from under the throne an enormous turd falls upon the sparkling new roof, shatters it, and breaks the walls of the cathedral asunder.'*
Carl Jung[19]

I'd only been a Curate for about two and a half years when I moved to my second post of Team Vicar. This meant having responsibility for the largest church in the County (after the Cathedral itself). It was a beautiful mediaeval Priory within a quaint market town near the Welsh border. I remained in that post for eight years and, though I will never regret the time, it ended up as the most disenchanting period of my life. Do not misunderstand me, I loved serving the church and town, and had the privilege of getting to know hundreds of angels both inside and outside the congregation. But there were underlying pressures against which I had little or no defence, some of them un-asked for and others of my own stupid making.

To be a Stipendiary Minister[20] today means not only being a pastor and a preacher but also an administrator and a manager, and to be blunt, I was utterly crap at the management stuff! The business-world demands on the modern clergy are impossibly high, especially when most of us were never trained to run a business. I admire every parish priest of the land who doesn't crack under the pressure, for they spin more plates than the average circus performer, as well as having to feed the spiritual needs of the community and offer pastoral care to all who come.

But I loved the people-stuff, particularly when it was out there in the community. I saw my most important function as being a pastor who was there to offer service and support to the 12,000 members of the local community – to bless their babies, join together their couples and bury their departed. As far as Church based things went I enjoyed preaching, leading services and creating imaginative rituals and ceremonies. However the committees, with all the in-house politics, the building upkeep, the legislation from above and all the damn paper work – yuk. I also found myself being easily bullied by some of the more powerful members of the congregation. For many of them I was simply not their idea of a clergyman. I didn't imagine it. I was told it on a regular basis - too young, too inexperienced, too worldly and far too vulnerable in the pulpit.

Churchgoers are generally not used to preachers talking about their doubts, questions and ups and downs, but I believe being honest about your faith and how you grapple with it is essential. The spiritual teachers who are most endearing are those who don't simply dish out all the platitudes and text book answers but admit to the fact that life is difficult and sometimes there simply *aren't* any answers. I always tried to be passionate in the pulpit, and one thing I was passionate for was a realistic faith. Just like my shop salesman days, I knew folk could smell bullshit. So my attitude was not to give the 'official' answers to theological questions but to look at beliefs from every angle and challenge them if they sounded like crap. This inevitably meant saying more than folk would usually expect from a clergyman.

I always viewed preaching as an awesome privilege, and my weekly periods of preparation became wonderful adventures where I would explore each and every question, problem and topic under the sun, with a view to sharing the results on Sundays. Often my talks would end up giving the congregations more questions than answers but, because I was prepared to be totally open and honest about my doubts as well as my beliefs, many warmed to them. I like to think of a sermon as an honest public conversation with myself, on which the congregation gets to eavesdrop. The risk, though, is that spiritual honesty means vulnerability and vulnerability, to some, is threatening! One Sunday morning a dear old lady came up to me after the service and said, 'Mark we do feel sorry for you.' I asked why and she said, 'Well you have such a lack of faith, and we all feel that if you could only have more faith, like us, you'd be a much happier person.' I was stunned. I didn't answer. I could have said that faith is not faith without doubt but, to be honest, she'd totally silenced me.

There were other problems in my life, not least the deep unhappiness at home, and within a few years I'd become engulfed in a black cloud of depression. It had attacked me before, but never to this extent. I sought medical help and was signed off work, put on anti-depressants, and allocated a counsellor. It's hard enough for someone in a regular job to admit to a so-called breakdown, but for a *clergyman!* Talk about humbling! The only thing worse was when I had to tell my congregation that my wife and I were going to divorce, which came a year or so after the breakdown. There's no need to go into the whys and ifs of that saga. It's enough to say that, like any separation (especially where children are involved) it was a painful and shattering experience.

I made some enormous mistakes during this period of my life. I was an utter fool in many ways, and allowed myself to act like an immature brat. This inevitably meant that people were disappointed and hurt. I am deeply sorry for that. However humans are speckled. None of us are perfect. And when the shit comes we're all capable of acting like rat bags.

Depression and disillusionment remained part of my life for quite a few years, though I was helped enormously by various counsellors and therapists throughout that time. One great lesson that kept coming to me [as if I had to *miss* the point again and again just so I could *get* the point again and again] was that often these dark nights of the soul can lead to new glimpses of light and creativity. So, scattered throughout these years were dozens of attempts to make use of the emotional pain by re-directing its energy into creative and imaginative innovations (again, both inside and outside the church). Some were quite radical, others were just mad. One of them, which was both radical and mad, was a huge fund raising event for the church. I'd always been charmed by the notion of medieval churches being places where more than just religion took place. Mystery plays, feasts and community celebrations all occurred within the sacred space of church buildings. So, dressed up as a fund raiser (at which it did rather well), was my attempt to re-create the medieval madness of the feast of fools. Being well aware of the fact that I was not the only vicar who had a party trick up his cassock sleeve I enlisted five others. The six of us, together with some fantastic folk from the community and congregation put on *Crazy Clerics – a Christmas show 'wiv' a difference.* Not only did it make about 2,500k, it filled the enormous Priory with people who would never normally set foot in the place. They laughed their heads off for two and a half hours solid.

Among the acts was a version of Monty Python's Holy Hand-Grenade of Antioch sketch, a priest-comic, a clerical-juggler, a vicar's impression of Pete and Dud and an auction of ridiculous Holy Relics. We even stopped to sing the congregational hymn *All Things Dull and Ugly* borrowed from the Python musical repertoire.

For the few weeks leading up to the event we sold Crazy Clerics merchandise after Sunday services, which included a variety of spoof religious artefacts, from 'Sacred Relics of the True Floss' to 'Happy Santcus Communion Wine (75% proof)'. Most people took it in the spirit it was intended, i.e. extreme blasphemy [only joking]. However I did overhear one elderly woman as she held an empty container labelled 'Genuine Priory Sacred Space': 'Well I never,' she said, shaking her head and peering at the item in her hand, 'They're even selling the air now.' I couldn't believe it either.

Other examples of my attempted innovations were not quite as mad but equally radical. One of the most exciting of these was what I called P.R.I.S.M. It stood for *PRIory Special Mass* and used the lovely image of a prism (the seven colours of the light spectrum all coming from pure white light) as a powerful symbol of the vastness and variety of global spirituality. We used incense, candles, coloured light, videos projected onto on huge screens, smoke machines, ambient music and basically anything we could get our hands on to add to the eclectic atmosphere. Though it was a Mass (Holy Communion) we also used prayers, readings and blessings from all traditions, inside and outside the Church. It proved to be enormously popular and attracted folk who'd been squeezed out of Christianity as well as some who had never attend any church before.

However, even with the success of Crazy Clerics and my other colourful introductions into church services, I was gradually losing faith in *Church*ianity. I didn't realise it then, but looking back, that's what it was - a gradual dissatisfaction with the whole world of institutional Christianity. The odd thing was that the more difficult I found church based things, the more wonder and beauty I saw in the world outside formal religion. I started to make more and more of the encounters I was having through, what some call 'folk religion'.

It always amazes me how the vast majority of people still seem to use the established religion of our land for 'occasional offices.'[21] But what amazes me more is the amount of clergy I come across who don't like doing baptisms, weddings and funerals, especially for non-church people. I have always seen them as an awesome privilege. As a vicar I went out of my way to create services, blessings, celebrations and rituals that were honest, meaningful and relevant for the folk who wanted them. If a deceased man was an atheist when he died, and his next of kin wanted to honour that, while also offering comfort to the few religious members of the family, then that would all be reflected in the ceremony. I would therefore be happy to make it as religious or secular as was necessary, and would use readings, prayers, blessings and music from every possible source – again secular or spiritual. What was of supreme importance, was not that I 'make sure I preach the gospel' but that the family's needs were totally respected.

Many clergy (and church goers in general) will disagree with what I have just written. Some will even see me as selling out to my own faith for not directly preaching the gospel at funerals. However I never held the view that one actually needs to *talk* about Jesus to make him present. If people from the local community chose to invite me to conduct their special ceremony then they knew what I represented. I was the vicar! To me that was enough. My role was to discover what their needs were and articulate them, by creating a suitable ritual that honoured both the deceased member of the family and the family themselves. Usually it would be 'loosely religious'; sometimes it would be non-religious yet spiritual; often it would be distinctively Christian. It all depended on the family's needs.

Of course, this might all seem obvious and expected, but I do know of some clergy who don't even allow particular hymns, prayers or spiritual readings at the funerals... because they 'don't agree with the theology'. The family might have come across a prayer before (perhaps at another family funeral) and wish to use it again, but are blatantly refused. Surely this is the one occasion where 'being theologically sound' is far less important than offering grace, love and compassion. I sometimes imagine a whole group of 'theologically sound' clergy jumping in Dr. Who's Tardis and zooming back in time to the scene of the Last Supper – the original Eucharist. They arrive and see a bearded man lift high the bread and wine and, just as he's about to say a blessing, one of the ecclesiastical know-alls blurts out, 'Hey, you can't do that. You haven't been validly ordained!'

The last funeral I ever conducted as a Vicar has always stood out as a powerful reminder of the importance to respect where folk are coming from. I was asked to create a service for the late husband of a woman who worked in one the town's metaphysical (New Age) shops. Her name was Maria. At first she was even unsure whether I'd allow her to use the church at all. She'd been refused the use of one (in another town) for her own marriage because of a previous divorce! I went to see her and, through many tears, she told me all about her beloved Cliff and their life together. Their home was full of all the wonderful artwork, imagery and interests they shared and, knowing how hard she was finding it, I suggested that we ought to make the ceremony an extravagant reflection of her husband's life. She warmed to the idea and the funeral turned out to be one of the most beautiful rituals I've ever been part of: not because of what I did, but because of what Maria allowed to happen.

Some time afterwards I met with a Clergyman (high up in the church) and told him about the service, explaining how deeply emotional it had been as Maria blew bubbles around Cliff's coffin and read to him.

'Oh, Mark,' he said, shaking his head, 'it really doesn't help you know.'

In fact it did help her and, since then, I've had opportunity to see Maria a few times. She obviously still finds the memories painful, but has moved on wonderfully. She is happy and free. She was also willing to offer a little piece for this book - something to help reinforce how important it is to take people and their lives seriously, to treat them with deep respect, and not to simply come from the perspective, 'No, I don't agree with the theology.'

Dear Mark,

Everything I have written is from my heart. It brought back tears and memories, but that alone has been healing for me, so Thank You. I truly feel that if you hadn't allowed me to include the lovely personal touches, within the funeral service, I would now be looking back at the funeral and feeling that I and The Church had let Cliff down.

I wish you happiness now and always.

With kindest wishes,

Maria.

## Maria's Thoughts

When my husband Cliff died in May 2007 I very much wanted a church service for him, as the Church of England had always been held in high regard by us both. Throughout my life the Church has always been a place of sanctity, peace and healing for me.

I didn't know what to do or who to turn to, so I rang the Priory vicarage and asked if I could speak to the Vicar. Mark returned my call and came out to visit me. It was a pure delight and relief to meet him. He showed such compassion and understanding, giving me totally unwavering support amidst my grief. He had many of the attributes that I had come to expect from a member of the clergy but there were other special qualities that he showed, qualities that can't be taught or learnt....and one of those was the quality of wanting me to feel that the church had given their love and blessing to whichever way I felt was best to honour my late husband.

During our conversation, Mark suggested that I might like to include some pieces within the service that would "bring to life" the man that Cliff had been and to enable all who attended the funeral service to feel close to him. I didn't know if I could include special items within the traditional funeral service that I felt would have honoured the man that Cliff had

been throughout his life, or to symbolise the love and togeth-
erness that we had shared. Mark assured me that whatever I
wanted could be included.

The funeral service that Mark conducted for my late
husband offered immense comfort and support to me,
allowing me to do certain things - like blow bubbles to the
heavens during the prayers (something that Cliff and I used to
do, having had them blown at our marriage ceremony too).
Mark also took a basket full of artistic and sacred items from
our home that included crystals, spiritual symbols, candles,
angels and Native American images. He decorated the entire
altar area with them and played Native American drumming
music as the coffin was brought into the church. This brought
Cliff's and my world directly into the heart of the sacred space
within the church which was so very important. Without these
touches and gestures I feel that it would have left quite a void
within the service. I was also allowed to read a prayer and
poem that I had written for Cliff. His stepson and friends also
had the opportunity to read poems and prayers that had been
collected from around the world. It softened the grief
somehow and enabled me to feel God's all encompassing love
and to feel that I had honoured Cliff in one of God's most Holy
places.

There could have been no greater comfort to myself, a
grieving widow, than to be allowed to have had the extra
touches added to the funeral service for my beloved husband,
within the parameters of the Church of England, especially
when I was supported, comforted and understood by a vicar
such as Mark.

When I look back at the service and the wonderful way
with which Mark conducted it for Cliff, I know that it was the
start of my healing from the severe pain and loss of my
husband. For me, I am utterly sure that Jesus would have been
very proud to have had Mark alongside Him. For Jesus

showed only love, compassion and understanding, just as Mark did to me and there can be no greater mark of respect that I could give Mark.

During the last few years of my ministry the more I got involved in life outside the church the more I managed to meet and befriend those members of the community who would never normally have any time for the religious establishment. My magic was a great bridge builder and, within a short time, I'd become know as 'the pub-priest' - the guy in the dog collar who could always be found down The Grapes with a beer in one hand and a deck of cards in the other.

Chapter 5

# The Three Magics - 2

*Throughout recorded history, the wonders of the conjurer's art have also been experienced both as the symbols and catalysts for experiences of wonder and enchantment. In this, the individual magic trick points beyond itself to a world in which enchantment is, to a world in which wonder and awe are necessary ingredients of a happy and healthy life.*
Eugene Burger[22]

As I took myself and my magic out from the church to the pubs, shops and streets, it started to take on a much more mysterious genre. This was due to the fact that my magic was becoming less 'prop orientated' and more 'mind based'. Most novice magicians begin with lots of magical apparatus (from big colourful vanishing bags to coins, cards and sponge balls) and then, over time, find their own particular performance style disregarding many of the previously acquired props. I began to develop an interest in the more mental form of the art which, if done well, can be incredibly powerful and can make the magic occur right inside the spectator's imagination rather than in the hands of the performer.

However, still being conscious that folk might misinterpret it, I continued to use a disclaimer: 'I'm not a real magician or a psychic!' I also became much more aware that I could use magic as a way of evoking genuine experiences of wonder and enchantment rather than just an illustrative tool. The following extract from a magazine article sums up what folk eventually thought of this eccentric priest:

You might catch a glimpse of him in the shadowy background of his local pub, encircled by a fascinated and enchanted group of onlookers. 'What's happening?' you ask.

'It's the Vicar', calls out the disinterested bar manager from across the room as he continues to wipe a beer glass dry. He's seen it all before... many times, but the crowd hasn't and neither have you. You step a little closer to the mystery. *Vicar? What does he mean, Vicar?* You push yourself through the crowd and see for yourself. *Oh my God!*

There, sat with his hand stretched out on the wooden table, is the cause of all the excitement. A figure dressed in black, with eyes half closed and a look of deep concentration on his face. You glance at all the expressions around the table. Their eyes are all focussed on the same place and you follow their gaze. Then you stop breathing for a moment. In the mysterious man's stretched out hand lies a spoon... but this spoon is moving. Damn it the spoon is curling upward as his hands stays still.

*Holy Sh\*t!*

You and the crowd continue to watch as he tips the spoon onto the table. One young woman reaches out. She seems to expect a shock as she delicately touches it with the tip of her finger. It's ok. She picks it up. It's passed round and eventually you handle it yourself. You try to bend it. *How the hell did he do it?*

For the next hour or so you are transfixed by the mysteries you witness right in front of your eyes. He makes objects move, plucks memories out of your mind, tells you what word you are thinking of and even brings tears to some spectators' eyes... tears, not of sadness, but the joy of re-discovering their enchanted inner child.

His magic is not like the conjuring tricks you've seen before. This guy seems different. He claims he is not psychic. He says it's a mixture of psychology, illusion and suggestion.

He claims he's not reading your mind but reading your personality from the subtle clues you give off. You don't know what to think and leave that night in an aura of spellbound wonder. You have touched a place within yourself that has not been visited for many years. Part of you wants to know how he did it but the bigger part wants to stay with the mystery.[23]

I have lost count of the times magic has led to a night of incredible discussions on life, the universe and everything – metaphysical conversations with complete strangers that a typical evangelist would die for (well perhaps not actually *die* for). But to me they were not about evangelism. It was a privilege to be welcomed into such personal areas of peoples' lives. To have folk open up to you about their deepest questions is a humbling experience. Of course I learned far more myself, from these late night bar sessions, than anyone else in the pub. Ordinary folk never cease to amaze me with what they know. Stumbling across natural wisdom is always enchanting.

What I noticed about my magic was that it seemed to have the power to quieten the overactive rational and critical mind (the left brain hemisphere) and bring to the surface the more intuitive and spiritually open part of the mind (the right brain hemisphere). Magical effects that have a mysterious edge are powerful placebos for a mind seeking enlightenment. A good magician, well practised in the art of performance, can genuinely bring wonder back to life. Whereas ill practised cheap tricks just leave audiences with a clever puzzle to solve and, rather than awakening the right brain, send the left brain into overdrive. This is what I recognise to be the second stage in my magical development – the use of magic, not just as an illustrative tool, but as an evoker of deep wonder and enchantment.

More and more my 'spiritual family' became the folk-world of those who hardly or never set foot inside the church. In many ways I was most alive in the context of this secular pub culture but, at the same time, I was lonely and sad. Why was my own religious community so hard to feel part of? Why was I so disconnected from my own faith? I loved my church on one level: its mess and muddle, its power to touch and bring hope to real people... screwed up and hurt people... people like me. Yet that very message – that the broken can be gathered, valued and helped back up by this messy-god-man – was simply not a message that I could relate to the middle class and perfectionist world of much C of E Christianity. It upset and frightened me that I was even beginning to see the Church as the antithesis of what I most loved about the original story. What had happened to the Jesus of the New Testament, who scooped up the marginalised, pointed to *them* and said 'the kingdom of God is *inside you*'? What had happened to the carpenter radical who challenged 'mainstream religiosity' and seemed to find more glory out in the gutter than inside the holy places?

# Chapter 6

# More Holy Sh*t

*Imagine stepping off a treadmill. You have been running on a treadmill for so long, but you have decided to step off. And now you are walking across the grass towards the edge of a great cliff, to leap into a gorgeous void. After so much meaningless and exhausting activity – for meaningless activity is particularly exhausting – you long to throw yourself into the strange holding of nothing. Will you dare?*

*The ego is running after you, telling you not to be so stupid, that you'd be mad to jump, to stay on the treadmill at all costs. He says you will kill yourself if you jump. He says there's nothing there. He asks how can you wish for nothing when the treadmill works so well?*

*What do you say? What do you do?*

Simon Parke[24]

I turned, looked my ego in the eye, winked... and jumped!

The story of Jesus begins in shit and ends in shit. In fact there's shit all the way through! If there *was* a historical birth scene in that 'Little Town of Bethlehem', would it really be like the good old fashioned nativity plays our kids star in, or the over-sanitised Christmas card images? Don't get me wrong, all these images add to the magical nature of Christmas, and I'm all for that, but we mustn't see them as real. No, the actual story is not so quaint. It is however deeply relevant, for it's about a poor and homeless human family ending up in nothing more than an animal shack. No comfortable room with a bed. Just some dirty straw and a bucket of water. No fresh clean sheets and a cot. Just some old rags and a food trough. Think about the image. Apart from the parents, whose eyes would have first glimpsed this little one? Not the shepherds, nor the Magi, but those of the ox, ass and probably a rat or two. This is fantastic. It's a marvellously messy and muddled up picture of a 'god who meets us in the shit' – divinity intertwined with the animal muck! How native! How Celtic! How wonderful!

And what about the wandering preacher's final hours? Well the story tells of a gruesome experience - one load of shit after another. He was betrayed, rejected, beaten, spat upon, humiliated and then killed in the ugliest way possible. And the period between birth and death was not much better. He was misunderstood, called names, chased out of town, viewed with suspicion and cursed with a group of total misfits who kept getting it wrong. This is a god-image who lives in the gutter rather than at the top of the ladder.

On top of this he also seemed to be able to single out other people who lived the shitiest lives - the beaten up by life, the marginalised, the unclean, the so called prostitutes and sinners. He befriended them with compassion and showed them a way out of their self-despising mess. And here's the *really* important part of the story. He didn't say 'join a religion'. He didn't say 'believe in this or that doctrine'. He would not even allow people to bow down to him, as if to say 'don't look at me either'. He enabled them to find a way out because he changed their view of the divine and he changed their view of themselves. He helped them to feel good about who they were - valued, special, loved.

The more I look at these stories (whether literally true or not) the more I see that Jesus was not a founder of a new religion but a corrector of a religious mindset that sets up obstacles between humanity and divinity. Jesus, and many other holy men, women, gurus and teachers through history, offer this wisdom – 'do not look at me, look to yourselves; the Kingdom of God (deity) is right there'. Monty Python's infamous hero Brian offers the same wisdom. 'You don't need me,' he implores the crowds, 'lead yourselves'. Yet his followers ignore his advice and do what many religious folk do – settle for projection instead and make him their salvation. It's easier that way. Richard Rohr often says that one of the most successful ways Christians have avoided doing what Jesus said was to simply worship him. It's easier to bow down and shout constant hallelujahs than to get our own hands dirty by following him out into the world of brokenness and mess.

Sometimes it seems as though Church is all about being good, respectable, pure, clean and holy. Yet the central image of the whole faith is a god-man who is born, lives and dies in shit. In Christianity there's been much 'in the world not of the world' mentality, which has led to an unhealthy dualism. I've heard Church leaders say, 'We Christians live in the light and we must remain in the light by not having anything to do with darkness, *for God cannot look upon darkness.*' If this is Christianity then it no longer works for me. But I do not believe it is for, surely, the whole point of this mythic masterpiece is that the divine is *not* separate from us, the divine is *not* afraid of darkness and messed up humans. The symbolic god-man Jesus shows us how to find the beauty - the hidden treasure - by looking right beneath our feet. If there is one phrase I could use to sum up the glory of the whole Christian gift it is *Transfigured Shit*. Honest and *real* spirituality is not primarily concerned with making folk 'good' but 'true' – which means acknowledging and befriending our shadows rather than repressing them. Simon Parke puts this powerfully:

> '... the concepts of good and bad will always be secondary to true or false. The human journey is primarily about becoming true, rather than good. Truth is primary to goodness, because without truth goodness can have no sense of what it is. Goodness imaged by the false is a most terrible thing. Hitler believed he was good to be saving Germany from Jews,

gypsies and homosexuals. Many others thought him good too. It is more important to be true than good.'[25]

All this now leads me to one of the most important parts of my whole story. I've always believed that one of the Church's primary functions is to do with embracing the fallen and dispensing grace. However the truth is that while priest Mark Townsend never had a problem with offering grace to other messy souls he just couldn't seem to do the same for himself. In the end the mess and unhappiness from his own journey proved too burdensome to be able to continue as a priest.

As I tell this part of my story it will be necessary for me to let out some 'stuff' that you might find uncomfortable. For me it is all deeply painful and rather humiliating but, in order to keep the book authentic, it must be said. On top of this there will, throughout the rest of the book, be extracts from my spiritual journal, some of which make me sound like I live constantly in 'victim' mode. There are a few examples of occasions where I come to the end of my own resources and sit – head in hands – up in my local forest, shaking my fist at life! In order to fully appreciate why I occasionally get to that 'place' I need to *show* what has happened, and it needs to be as transparent as possible. I am even more convinced of this after having receiving a letter from a trusted friend who did me the honour of reading the first draft of the book.

I'm fortunate to have some extremely wise and helpful friends – many of whom have helped me with the proof-readings and general criticisms of this book. One such person is the remarkable Mentalist (or thought reader) Drew McAdam. For those unfamiliar with stars of the magic world you might be more likely to recognise him as *The Interrogator* from the hugely popular Trisha show. Drew used to work within military intelligence and is an expert at routing out in-authenticity and dishonesty. I was delighted when he said he'd like to read my book and equally delighted by his response which, in typical Drew fashion, was constructive and critical.

'...I need to like the person in a book. It's one of the golden rules of any book, really. Because if you LIKE the person, then you care what happens to them. And I DID like the Mark in the book – the one who wore strange clothes. The one who put the Sex Pistols record on the turntable. "Spare a talent for an ex-leper" Brilliant. I wanted to know this guy. I was WITH him.

However, the guy who sits miserable in the woods after the most crushing period of his life etc.? I'm not so keen on him. And the reason I'm not so keen on him is because I don't know him. I don't know what happened. I don't know how he got to that point. And I firmly believe the reader needs to know what happened. I'm sorry if that sounds brutal, but we need to know! I want him telling his story, but making light of it at the same time. I want to hear the voice of the young joker Mark getting himself into trouble.

Sure, it's probably dark. You SAY it is, but SHOW me! That way, the revelations will have so much more meaning as I struggle with you and feel that we are walking into the light together. You are taking the reader with you. If I really know the crushed, disappointed, frightened little-boy Mark, then I care about him and can celebrate with the Mark who has left that place behind. You have taken me on a journey. Make me realise that, in the same circumstances I would have made the same choices - and would have produced the same results. Maybe you feel shame at the mistakes... so what? Be honest with the reader. We've all made mistakes; that's why we are reading the book!

Put more of yourself in there – the autobiographical accounts gives us understanding as to how you came to think the way you do. And that really SELLS it to us. (I suppose it's a little bit the way we "sell" a magic trick to our audience – by putting ourselves in there. Therein lies the magic.)'

Wonderful and wise words aren't they? So here goes.

In May 2007 my beautiful fiancée and I were busy preparing for what are commonly seen to be three out of the top five highest causes of stress (wedding, new job, new home). I'd met Jodie quite early in my priestly career. In fact her grandma's funeral was one of the first I ever performed as Team Vicar. But it was not until New Year's Day of 2006 that we 'got it together' *romantically*. The few years before that had been a mess for both of us and, in my case, a nervous breakdown, intense periods of heavy counselling, AA meetings, destructive relationships and massive amounts of self-doubt. Throughout these years I'd tried my best to continue serving God and church, but stumbled from one disaster to another, all of which I take full responsibility for.

Consequences follow actions. It's one of life's most basic laws. We reap what we sow. This is one major reason why I refuse to hold on to the petty grudges and feelings of hostility towards those who've hurt me. Revenge is like drinking rat poison in an effort to kill the damn rodent. Venom, let loose, will only end up poisoning ourselves.

But I didn't need rat poison to hurt me – I had a habit of turning my anger and pain inward anyway. So I decided to do something very risky... to put my money where my mouth was and unburden myself not to another anonymous counsellor, family member or friend, but to someone within the ecclesiastical world whose opinion I would have no option but to take note of. I needed to be brave enough to share all my shit and mess with this person and not only that, do whatever he recommended. That was my condition to myself.

So I was about to move to a new post within the church, taking my new wife Jodie with me. But my heart told me I needed to do something before I could feel free to be Installed.[26]

It all has to do with that word authenticity again. In order to be made the new Priest in Charge, I would have to go through a ceremony where, among other things, I would be required to submit to the authority of both the Bishop and the Queen (Church and State). The Bishop would end the ceremony by giving me his blessing for my future as someone who shared his 'cure of souls'. Both my previous Installation ceremonies were under the former Bishop's reign.

Well, my heart simply would not let me go through all this until I'd looked my Bishop in the eye and allowed him to see the 'real Mark'. I knew that I would need to make something of a confession to him, and tell him about all the mess and muddle of the previous few years. There was literally no other way. I do believe in transparency, especially within the context of such situations as this. The problem was that one particular part of this mess was 'big stuff'. Sure, I'd talked it through (and even made confessions) many times before (even to the church hierarchy) but this man was my new Father in God. I simply could not stand before him, feel his hand of blessing on my head, and know that my sorry story was a secret.

Not only did I ask the advice of Jodie (who was with me all the way), I also sought council from half a dozen or so trusted friends in dog collars. Only one of them thought I should do it – my dear best man. The rest said that, while my 'mess' was something that probably a quarter of the clergy of the land had (at some point) made, there was no point bringing up the past when it could threaten my future. I disagreed. A future would be no future at all if it were not authentic. I needed to risk everything in order to gain freedom. The freedom might have also included a new post in the country or it might not.

Thus a week and a half before my wedding I sat in front of my Bishop and made what was essentially an informal confession about my past. I cannot tell the whole tale here for it is not mine alone to tell. However I can say that some of it was do to with a relationship I'd gotten into with a married woman who (at the beginning) was still living with her husband. It had begun quite a few years previously, back when my first marriage had come to such a miserable end, but it was all well and truly over by the time I'd started dating Jodie (on New Year's Day of 2006).

To this day I am deeply ashamed of what I did, and am truly sorry for the obvious pain I caused. But we humans are a mixture of light and dark. And when life gets hard, and dreams are shattered, we can react in foolish and selfish ways. I was messed up and allowed myself to get attached to a sympathetic soul, but it was wrong and I take full responsibility for my actions – *which is why I never ended up moving to that new post.*

My Bishop listened to my story, and showed immense sympathy for me. He ended by thanking me for sharing what I had, saying a prayer and giving me a hug.

I drove home feeling liberated and thought that was it! I told Jodie and my clergy counsellors that it was all ok. So it was on with the wedding plans. Then, a day before the Big Day, I had a phone call. It was my Bishop. He needed to see me again – urgently. I arrived at the Palace and sat in his chapel as the poor man told me how anguished he'd been since our last meeting. He asked my permission to talk it through with his assistant Bishop and Archdeacon, and said he would need to see Jodie and I together after we had returned from our honeymoon.

Please understand. I need to express this here because when it comes to the extracts from my journal, you will at least understand why it sometimes sounds so dark and dramatic. While my honesty to the Bishop was liberating, the practical and emotional consequences have been crippling.

The wedding day was beautiful. But both of us had all this on our minds. Likewise our honeymoon was simultaneously joyful and painful. What the hell were we going back to?

Then we were back and sat in front of the Bishop! We listened as we heard him tell us that he could not, in conscience, licence me to the new post, and that I would not be able to apply for a position as a Priest for at least three years. He and his colleagues thought it was the only way. I can't pretend it wasn't a bombshell. Even though we knew that this was a potential, both Jodie and I thought it would all be ok. Personally something inside me still held hope that forgiveness and grace, new beginnings and clean slates followed confession and repentance. I would have understood more if Jodie had, *herself*, been something to do with the original break up of my first marriage, but she had not. I had not begun my relationship with her until I was free from *all* other romantic attachments!

On the other hand I'd put the Bishop in a very difficult position and I did respect the toughness of his approach. I'm not writing any of this because I have any blame towards anyone (apart from myself). The reason for allowing this part of the story to have a place is so that the rest of the book rings true and is authentic. *My* mistake all those years ago, and *my* decision to let my boss know about it, changed the very shape of my future. Not only that, it changed Jodie's and my children's too. I still hold on to the fact that truth is the better way. If I could go back to that week and a half before my wedding, I'd do the same thing again.

There is a biblical saying: 'The truth shall set you free'. Some say the original meaning is closer to 'reality shall set you fee'. For me, at first, it felt like 'the truth has ruined my life'. But over time I realised that true freedom is about honesty. I could not live in a world of falseness and pretence, even if it were a dream-like existence of luxury and bliss. I was going to take my wife and children to a new life in the country, serving a group of small villages and living on the edge of a forest in a massive detached vicarage. I now live in an ex-council house, with barely enough money to pay the bills, but I am free - oh God I am free!

So I was suddenly faced with the problem of not knowing what to do with my life... and, more urgently... how to make a living, especially as I was newly married, and had two dependent children living with me for three days each week. Almost immediately [perhaps it was shock] my imagination started talking: 'Mark, this is what you've been waiting for – a kick up the arse to do something you've dreamed of for years – become a full time spiritual magician.' But, just as quickly, I came back to reality. I needed to think quickly about the here and now. What the hell was I going to do about money? Then another flash of inspiration came: 'Get a cleaning job.' Jodie had an embryo cleaning company and was always looking for an extra pair of hands so, after discussing it, we agreed to take seriously *both* my ideas. I would work as a cleaner and, at the same time, try to set up as a full time magician. Then, once I was established and making enough money from magic, I could let go of the cleaning.

Within just a month I'd exchanged my cassock, dog collar and communion vessels for an apron, vacuum cleaner and bog brush. One minute I was pastor of the biggest church in the County and the next I was cleaning peoples loos. How humbling, but how wonderfully life changing too. On the one hand nothing could adequately describe the anguish and fear of those months, but on the other it was all so liberating. For years I'd spent almost every waking moment planning the next thing – sermons, meetings, services, catching up on official paperwork and so on. But now, with just a whole load of homes to clean, the tensely wound up spring in my head started to uncoil. There were still big things [huge things, like where the hell were we going to live] to worry about, but no more constant planning, planning, planning. In a strange way scrubbing loos and ironing was therapeutic and freeing. Looking back I would describe the six or so months I spent cleaning as a gift. I can't say I could have done it forever, but those months simply concerned with manual chores gave my overactive mind a break. It was almost meditative. Like a mantra.[27] I also learned much about service. For years I'd 'served' as a priest in an institution who's founder washed his own followers' feet. Oh we would imitate that once a year on Maundy Thursday but it often came across more like a dramatic production than a real act of humble service. To scrub real loos was a taste of servanthood.

Another huge problem we faced after everything changed was where were we going to live? We were kindly offered a church house to rent, with a few months at a reduced rate, but when back up to the full price, and we'd added on the other costs involved in heating, lighting and paying council tax for a massive old county vicarage... it would have been impossible. Plus there was no guarantee that it would be our home for more than a year, and with both of us setting up new businesses this would have been mad.

In the end we were forced to do something not just mad but crazy... something neither of us ever dreamed we would have been forced to do. With the financial help of both sets of parents, we bought a house *totally blind*. By that I mean we bought a house without even looking at it. It was a bargain but, because of a certain 'history' between the tenants and my wife, we could not let it be known that we were interested. That saga was a complete nightmare. Every time we were told the house would be vacated, something happened to make it all go wrong. Meanwhile the church needed back the one we were still living in. I resigned in June 2007 and the house we were buying did not officially become vacated until the very end of the year. We could not actually move in until March 1st 2008.

Thankfully, my sister-in-law came to the rescue. She and her fiancé had just bought a house in the town and, postponing their own move, graciously allowed us to rent their new home over the winter months.

All in all the amount of extra shit [and I've not mentioned all of it] that came our way during the first year of our marriage was a nightmare. No wonder we often feel like we've not yet had a honeymoon period. No wonder it has, at times, been so difficult for us. It really was not a good situation for a newly married couple but, again, I take the responsibility for that.

Will I ever go back to the church's official ministry? Could I see myself as a vicar again? As a sit here now I can apply for a post in eighteen months time and, by the time this book has been published, that will be down to six months. At first I thought I would go back. I still have so much to offer! But now, in truth, I really don't think so. I have seen wonderful things over the last couple of years, things I would not have come across were I still a Vicar. My whole universe has expanded. I really don't think I could squeeze my view of life, deity, humankind or the spiritual world into a religious organisation again. I will always love the dear old C of E. And I will never stop admiring the founder of the Church. I know I'll also remain ever grateful for the many angels I've had the privilege of meeting through it. But no – now my quest moves me forward in a new direction. I've stepped through a door into a brand new vision of life. A vision far too exciting to turn back.

# Part 2

# 'Into the Realm of the Ravens'

## You were Meant to be Here – Ideas on the Spiritual Life

*You were meant to be here.*

*The source of life is pure limitless love.*

*Life is meaningful and your life has purpose.*

*All religions and spiritual paths are leading towards the same goal.*

*At the heart of the spiritual life is the search for wisdom and compassion.*

*Spirituality isn't just self serving… it's about being of value to other people and the world too.*

*You can make a difference.*

*These are critical times… the earth and humanity face challenges they have never faced before.*

*You don't need to worry about these challenges, but you shouldn't ignore them either.*

*The world is more mysterious and magical than you can possibly imagine.*

*You are not alone.*

*None of this belongs to you, and that is good.*

*You are whole and you are free.*

*Only sometimes you think or feel you are not.*

*You are the creator of your destiny.*

*The more you understand about how life works the more your can be of use to yourself and others.*

*You created your reality, but other people help create it too, just as you help to create their reality.*

*We're in this together, everything is connected.*

*You need to learn how to let go… how to be open, relaxed and unattached.*

*Your heart knows.*

*Deep down you know where you should be headed, and what you need to do.*

*Spiritual practise can help you hear the still small voice of your heart so that you can follow your bliss.*

*You don't need to wait to do any of this.*

*Life isn't a rehearsal this is it!*

*Be here... now!*

Text gathered and edited by Philip Carr-Gomm[28]

# Chapter 7

# Punch drunk on pagan hospitality!

*The raven shows us how to go into the dark*
*of our inner self and bring out the light of our true self;*
*resolving inner conflicts which have long been buried.*
*This is the deepest power of healing we can possess.*
Lin Oberlin

Notes from my journal (6 months after my 'ecclesiastical departure'):

*11<sup>th</sup> Jan 08 – I don't know how long the feeling will last but I can't*
*remember this kind of inner freedom. On the one hand money is*
*impossible and life is fragile, but I feel free, alive, unrestrained.*
*Problems still occur on a daily basis and certain people seem to have*
*a desire to make themselves my enemies. But I have no regrets and*
*could not now imagine putting back on the ecclesiastical straight-*
*jacket. The Christ spirit is still within me but now I am outside the*
*institution.*

*This morning, while I walked our German shepherd, was a*
*moment of natural magic. The sun still hid behind the hills and the*
*moon glowed with a shiny silver complexion. Stars twinkled and*
*glistened, and every so often a crow's call echoed through the*
*darkness. I felt my heart being drawn closer and closer to what some*
*call the pagan way.*

*I closed my eyes and looked with the imagination: The blue raven*
*calls. She beckons me to follow. Where does she fly? She flies*
*North... towards the snowy mountain peaks. She is a black dot in a*
*vast blanket of white... Her call is comforting in the loneliness – she*
*leads me on to places of uncharted territory. The blue raven is a bird*

*of exquisite grace and beauty. She is my soul calling me home. The blue raven's path is a passageway home to the true self. She is my animal spirit, my Jungian anima, my 'Pullmanian' deamon, my soul-guide. She marks my initiation as I step through the magic wardrobe – into a re-enchanted universe.*

Towards the end of 2007 my magical performances became a little more regular and I was able to gradually let go of a certain amount of cleaning work. Then I received a booking that was to dramatically change my life! That December I was invited by Philip Carr-Gomm, chosen chief of the Order of Bards, Ovates and Druids (OBOD), to speak and perform at the Order's Winter Gathering in Glastonbury. I'd always adored Glastonbury, my first visit being well over a decade before. I've always appreciated its unique ability to embrace spiritual traditions that are often seen as polar opposites, even enemies. On my visits – even while being a fully convinced C of E Priest - the magical town whispered secrets into the ears of my soul and re-kindled the smoldering ashes of my childhood interest in magic. I often used to return wondering if my heart was really half way between the two worlds of Christianity and Paganism.[29] Once, while still a curate in my first post, I felt inspired enough by the Glastonbury Pagan scene to preach a sermon entitled 'Christ and the Corn King,' which was an early attempt to try and understand some of the many crossovers between Christianity and our British Pagan past.

But now I was to perform in front of 200 or so pagans. Help! I'm usually nervous when performing – but 200 pagans! For at least ten years I'd respected and appreciated their world, but I was also aware that some (maybe many) pagans were, understandably, more than a little suspicious of Christians. It is not uncommon for a modern day pagan to come across a well meaning evangelist who feels its his duty to offer his 'services' - which could be anything from a quiet word of scriptural warning to a full blown exorcism. Apparently that very Somerset town had, only months earlier, been paid a visit by a particularly extreme Christian group, some of whom strutted into shop doorways throwing salt as a sign of deliverance, others who evangelized the streets. I did not want to be seen as an evangelist in disguise. I did not see the invitation as an opportunity to push my faith. I saw it no differently to how I see any such invitation: an opportunity to share magic and evoke the experience of deep enchantment. I was not prepared for the life-changing encounter that awaited me!

I walked into the huge Town Hall, where the Druids were assembled. It was decorated with bright and colourful banners of the various Groves[30] and bunches of hanging mistletoe. The audience were an eclectic mishmash, some of whom could have been my middle-class grandparents, others who had a more stereotypical pagan look - women in crushed red velvet dresses, and beautiful long flowing hair; men in cloaks and hats decorated with green leaves. The speaker, who had the fixed gaze of every single eye, could have been a tutor from Hogwarts, with his red lined long black robe and dandy white ruffed shirt billowing out from underneath. He looked fabulous. It turned out we'd met before – he and I – a long time before. Back in the days when I was planning to train as a Pentecostal pastor I paid a visit to the Bible College up in Nantwich, Cheshire. My own church's assistant pastor-to-be was there, finishing his studies, and he'd agreed to show me round. One of the College students was the very speaker on the Glastonbury stage, Kristopher Hughes. He now leads a Druid community on the sacred Isle of Anglesey. Filled with Welsh passion and irreverent humour his talk was energetic, inspiring and hilarious.

At the interval I took the opportunity to find Philip Carr-Gomm and introduce myself. Philip is an amazing man. He oozes genuine warmth and has a deeply spiritual air, though without any pretension or pomposity. I found him to be charming, cheerful, and welcoming. He told me what he wanted of me and I took the opportunity to get him to secretly draw me a simple picture and seal in an envelope. I asked him to keep hold of it as I might make use of it later in my slot on stage.

The next lecture was a fascinating potted history of the Order of Bards, Ovates and Druids by the enigmatic and impressive pagan scholar Professor Ronald Hutton. And after that Philip took the platform and introduced his mystery guest – a vicar who also does magic!

It was a wonderful experience. Every performer knows when an audience is with them, and this lot were with me. They trusted me and warmed to the message I presented. I did various mind-reading stunts, even managing to duplicate a secret drawing of the chosen chief himself! I also had some fun with an effect I often use in churches, usually calling it Denominational Hats. The normal procedure is to get four volunteers up on the stage and hand them a blank card on which they are asked to write the name of a colour which most symbolizes God. But to make it more interesting each of the four volunteers must represent a different tradition within the church. I often use high-church, low-church, broad-church and Christo-pagan, the latter usually taking the most time to find a willing volunteer. Once each volunteer has written down their colour, and the cards have been adequately mixed, I then see if I can decipher which colour goes with which person / denomination. It's a fascinating exercise in colour psychology. However, for these pagans I clearly had to do something different. So, I began by asking how many of the audience were once part of a Christian denomination? Well over 100 hands willingly shot up. Then I broke down the 100 into various denominations – Catholic, Pentecostal, Anglican etc. Finally I asked for three volunteers who could try to represent their original Christian tradition and one could represent a fully pagan tradition. Once up on stage I asked each to write down the colour that most represents god, goddess, spirit or deity, after which I correctly discerned whose was whose.

My final effect was more of a traditional magic-trick. It's how I often close a performance. I make a paper doily snow flake by cutting random holes in a folded up tissue and, as I'm doing so, talk about the symbolic nature of snow:

'Did you know that a snowflake is a mirror? A tiny snowflake is a reflection of the human soul. If you really look at the leaf of ice that lands on your palm you will see the creative design – a unique and beautiful pattern that is once only... it will never exist again in that form. It is perfect and precious as it is. It is like all other snow flakes, for it is made of the same substance, but it is unlike all others because it has its own special mark, like the finger prints on your hands...

So, when you next see the first few flakes of winter snow floating down from the sky above, don't just rush to thoughts of snowballs or stuck cars... think deeper.... Think first of your own uniqueness and then the uniqueness of every other human soul... and thank God/dess for your place within this remarkable world-wide family. '

As I say those final words I crumple up the paper snowflake, take out an oriental fan, and create a gust of wind beneath the tissue. Suddenly a great cloud of snow bursts out of my hand and covers the front few rows of the audience. It is a beautiful sight and a fitting end to a symbolic magic show.

I left the platform with the little snowy symbols of human beauty and magic still drifting down from the ceiling. But what happened next was the real magic of the day. One after another, members of the order stepped forward to show their appreciation. I was greeted warmly when I first entered the building two hours previously. But no one knew I was a Christian vicar then. For all they knew I was a pagan. But now they knew the truth – I was a bloody vicar. The warmth was tangible.

I stayed for the rest of the day, and well into the night, speaking to lots of members of the Order. I know I shouldn't but

I can't help wondering what the welcome would have been like should the roles have been reversed. Imagine, a group of Christians are on their annual convention and they just find out that the speaker/performer is a pagan. My hope would, of course, be that he or she be offered the same open armed hospitality as I was, but is that realistic? I'll leave that for you to consider.

The next morning I traveled home in a daze. I'd spent the previous day and night in deep philosophical discussion but without the heavy theological debate one often finds when discussing spiritual things. The fact was that I'd felt at home there. I'd felt embraced, held, enfolded by the community – and in no sense proselytized or corrected. I had been taken for who I was. I'd even felt comfortable to share the whole story of how my life as a Vicar came to an end... *all of it*. I was listened to, accepted, and made to feel totally at home. It was genuine. That's why my head was a daze... punch drunk on delicious pagan hospitality.

One of the most impressive things I learned about my new friends, and their spiritual community, was that there were no set doctrines or dogmas. I even met a few other Christians there, only they were also long term members of OBOD. I have since learned that there are OBOD druids who are also members of almost every other religious or spiritual path. In fact there are even atheist members. It is a truly eclectic organization – which is bound to attract a good old universalist like me.

By the time I got home I knew the encounter was not a one off. It was the beginning of something... a new phase... a new quest even! In fact it was the same quest for enchantment, but I instinctively felt I had found a new path on which to travel - as if someone had turned on the lights. I'd opened a door in a magical old wardrobe and was about to walk through. The raven spirit was beginning to stir!

Good old Google! I spent the next few weeks using the faithful search engine to dig up all things druidic. I also ordered a pile of books from Amazon. Part of my search uncovered the exciting fact that OBOD offers a specially designed home study training course for those who want to learn more about druidic philosophy, faith and practice. It is divided into three Grades and often takes members over ten years to fully complete. Though intense it is non-dogmatic and can be used in whatever way a member wishes. The course is divided into three stages that correspond with the three traditional divisions of the ancient Druids: Bards, Ovates and Druids. Concerning the first Grade the Order's website states:

'The Bardic grade takes you on a journey through the cycle of the year, and introduces all the basic concepts of Druidry - showing you how it is a living Way that can be practised in the modern world, bringing a greater sense of connection with all of nature, and with the ancient heritage of the Druid wisdom-tradition.

The aim of the Bardic course is to help your life flourish and blossom - to help your Soul express itself fully in the world. It does this by helping you discover the sources of your creative power, so that their gifts can flow fully in your life. In addition, it teaches the fundamental skills and techniques of Druid spirituality - the use of ritual, of sacred space, of the circle, the directions and elements. During the first year you are taught thirteen rituals in addition to the eight Druid seasonal ceremonies. These rituals help to attune you to the natural world, to the rhythms of the earth and moon, the sun and stars. And as they do this, they help you to access your Deep Self - your Soul - that part of you which feels at one with all life.'[31]

Learning that I could subscribe to this course and, at the same time, have no pressure to change my faith or cease being a Christian made it quite impossible not to sign up immediately.

As I write these words I am not even a year into it. Therefore, rather than attempt to describe my own Bardic / Druidic journey, which would most certainly be both unassimilated and inexperienced, I decided to invite a number of other folk to describe their journeys into druidry. These folk have been walking the path for many years and are therefore much more qualified to tell their tales and express actual druidic teaching and philosophy. Their stories make up the third part of this book. For the next few chapters of the current section I will share some of the enchanting experiences that have come my way since stepping through that doorway into a world rich with natural magic.

# Chapter 8

# The Jesus-Tree and Nature's Cathedral

*We speak of mysteries in our squawks*
*And magic in our chatters*
*If you would slow*
*To natures ebb and flow*
*You would hear what really matters*
'Raven Talk' by Madeleine Walker, Animal Communicator

*The forest is not merely an expression or representation of*
*sacredness,*
*nor a place to invoke the sacred; the forest is sacredness itself.*
*Nature is not merely created by God, nature is God.*
Richard Nelson[32]

As I sit here, punching away at the computer keyboard, I can see my bookshelves in front of me and something about them stands out!

When we moved house a year ago, we had to squeeze a large detached vicarage-full of belongings into a small semi-detached ex-council house. On top of that were all my wife's items that had been in storage. It was an almost impossible task but we did it. One of the hardest things for me was pruning away about 85% of my library. My God it hurt. I love books and I'd gathered an impressive collection that filled my enormous vicarage study. They represented a 30-year spiritual journey. I still had my collection of Unexplained Magazines, all bound into neatly encased volumes. Somehow they'd escaped the flames of my over-zealous book burning sessions. As far as the Christian category went I had everything from popular evangelical novels about the 'end times' to the dense and heavy academic tomes of liberal theology and biblical critical scholarship. There were also many dozens of liturgical books representing the Catholic and Orthodox traditions as well as a huge amount of various Christo-spiritualities: charismatic, monastic, Celtic etc. On top of those were more than a few by Christian spiritual teachers who'd somehow managed to combine their own deep Christian vision and experience with other paths: Hindu, Buddhist, African, Native American and Celtic etc. And there were the books and pamphlets from outside the Christian world altogether. Most of these I'd managed to collect since the 'opening-up-period' of my Aston Training days. They represented various forms of Paganism, Greek mythology, Buddhism, Hinduism, Gnosticism, Psychology, Quantum Science and what's loosely referred to as New Age.

As I now ponder the few shelves that are left, it becomes quite obvious that the vast majority of the 85% that I let go of were 'Christian' and that most of the remainder are not. Something else strikes me. My interest in non-Christian spirituality goes back much further than I thought. I can see a copy of Principles of Paganism by Vivianne Crowley that I bought about a decade ago, and behind me are books on Eastern Spirituality and New Age that I bought well over fifteen years ago!

As far as Christian books go, I still own a few dozen but they generally tend to be of the 'spirituality' genre and have a highly inclusive / eclectic approach. For example my favourite Christian teacher, Fr. Richard Rohr, who passionately reminds us of the hidden treasures within Christianity, also draws on the rich wells of both Eastern Mysticism and Native American wisdom. I have books by other Christian guides who are heavily influenced by world spirituality: Brother John Martin Sahajananda (Christian-Hindu), John O'Donohue (Christian-Celtic), Anthony De Mello (Christian-Buddhist-Hindu), Sr. Elaine McGuiness (Christian-Zen), Bede Griffiths (Christian-Hindu), Christopher Bryant

(Christian-Jungian) and many others.

In truth noticing the eclectic and universalistic nature of my dishevelled bookshelves does not surprise me for, though I have always loved the person of Jesus, I have found Christianity to be less and less spiritually appealing and harder to make sense of intellectually.

Over the last few years I've grown to love many teachers of the eastern spiritual world, but something stops me going the whole way and becoming a Buddhist. The same is true for the more New Age western world. Books by the astonishing Vietnamese Zen Master and Peace Activist Thich Nhat Hanh remain breath-taking and beautiful treasures among my collection, as do the writings of Eckhart Tolle and Neale Donald Walsh. In many ways these books (which represent both East and West) say what I have always tried to express. But there is a word I often come across that always seems to be the place I get stuck - illusion. Of course as an illusionist I use the word to mean unreal – like a mirage. And in essence, when spiritual writers use the term they too mean 'what is unreal'. Much about our lives is deeply unreal. Much about our assumptions, dreams - even parts of our own characters - is unreal and illusory. However where I get stuck is that sometimes the whole world, the physical universe itself, is viewed as an illusion / unreal. I realise I have failed to adequately understand the term illusion when used this way, and I also know there are many different schools of thought within the spiritual worlds just mentioned, but it does sometimes sound as if, while Christianity teaches us to be 'in the world but not of the world', the Eastern and some parts of the New Age worlds often teach us 'to ascend [the illusion of] the world'.

Whenever I try to view the world as an illusion I find myself getting depressed. I prefer to see the world, the physical world around us, as a beautiful (and at times ugly) gift. I see it as the garment worn by deity. I see it as of immense value and importance *in itself*. I do not want to ascend it or rise above it. I want to be fully plugged into it.

While appreciating that countless millions have found true happiness and bliss by changing their perspective of the world and seeing it as unreal, I simply cannot do this. Perhaps it's my weakness. Perhaps some day I will follow this path. Perhaps I'm not ready for it yet. I'm certainly not saying it's wrong. Likewise I am not saying that the 'in the world but not of the world' view of Christianity is wrong. It's simply that I have found the nature-based view of a 'living' world, as being much more helpful. It makes far more sense to me right here right now.

In the Spring of 2008 I jotted down the following notes in my Journal. I'd been thinking about nature and the cosmos, in relation to general spiritual traditions. In my own limited way I'd discerned three broad categories of understanding. What was really interesting for me is that I seemed to feel closer to the third one on the list:

*The 3 approaches / paths:*

*Western religious (Judeo-Christian). This approach is often heavily dualistic, earth and matter denying. Humans are the Lord's of creation. There tends to be a big emphasis on 'The Flesh' and 'Sin' etc. There is also an underlying deep seated suspicion of 'the world'. We are in the world but we are not of the world.*

*Eastern Philosophical (Hindu, Buddhist, even Gnostic). I have many books that represent this tradition, and some are priceless jewels of wisdom. However this approach is sometimes (strangely) dualistic yet claimed to be non-dualistic. The most extreme versions can end up viewing the material world with almost the same kind of 'gotta get out of it' as the extreme Christian approach. The material universe is Maya – illusion. While I find the notion of non-attachment very helpful, I cannot see the earth beneath my feet as mere illusion to be woken up out of.*

> *Nature based (Celtic, Native American, and Aboriginal). These indigenous paths usually see the world as somehow divine in itself. It is sometimes Pantheistic, or sometimes Panentheistic, and usually Animistic. Everything has a spirit, an energy, a soul. The Earth is our Mother and the Sky is our Father. This tradition makes more and more sense to me.*

However, I still find great value in the term 'illusion' when applied to our thoughts, to what we believe about ourselves, what is unreal about ourselves. In the past I've used the term 'illusion' myself, in talks and writings. But I have always used it as a term to describe the dream-like state from which spirituality helps us to wake up. When we wake up we see ourselves and the world as it truly is, we become present to the moment and sense the deep connection of all things. For me these moments are priceless glimpses into the beauty and spiritual resonance of everything around us, so that the physicality of the planet is made even more real rather than less real. I do not see the physical world as an illusion in the sense that some spiritual teachers do, a mask, or even a veil to the true nature of every-thing. I see the physical planet as a beautiful gift *in itself.*

An ancient Christian doctrine that I have always appreciated is The Incarnation. Traditional Christianity understands this as the becoming flesh of God, the place where God literally steps into our world in the form of one man. However I have grown to see it as a symbol of *what already is*, as if there is a hidden divinity to humankind itself. So Jesus somehow represents what is true for all humans, and perhaps for the *whole of nature too* - that God lives in it and through it. I do not want to think of myself as 'not of the world' or as having to 'ascend the world'. I want to be fully part of it. And, as time has progressed, this is precisely what has been happening to my experience.

Over my last few years (as a Vicar) I started to recognise a gradual shift in how I understand the central facets of the faith to which I belonged. Being a free thinker, I was never really concerned about where my thoughts and ideas were going, as long as I was honest with myself. It seemed to be the case that, alongside both my theoretical fascination with other spiritual paths and my tendency to spend more and more real-time finding glimpses of God outside the church, came an automatic inner re-evaluation of belief. I remember sitting down, journal in hand, asking myself what the various doctrines and ideas of my own faith meant to me. I began with the Sacraments[33] and without thinking I wrote that they were simply beautiful ritual acts that dramatise and symbolise what is *already true*. For example, a baby's baptism might traditionally be seen of as some strange ceremony that brings a child out of darkness into light. But for me it was an acting out of what is already true for that child - he /she is *already* filled with divinity and is a child of God. Of course baptism is so much more than any words can describe which is why we use religious symbolism. Symbols speak a broader, more universal language than any verbal dialect. The real power of baptism is in the symbol of being buried and risen which, of course, will happen time and time again throughout life. In life we go through many deaths, be it a death of a career, a relationship or a literal death. Jesus (like the many god-man-Christ-figures before him) is, in part, a powerful symbol of what is true for all humankind – life, death, re-birth. Baptism acts this cycle out, which is why it appears in many other ancient cultures beyond the world of Christendom. Jung would possibly call it a universal archetypal ritual.

What about marriage? Well at a wedding the Priest's words do not *create* a married couple. In fact the couple themselves are the *real* priests in the marriage ceremony. It is their vows and their sexual joining together that *makes true what already is*. The ordained priest or celebrant merely vocalises and witnesses the event.

At a Eucharist [and here is where I'm likely to be accused of sacramental heresy] the priest, by ritual and drama, makes present the memory of something both shocking and wonderful that happened many years ago. The truth of this act is hard to fully comprehend [indeed there are possibly many truths] and the ritual enacted brings it to mind again. The most basic meaning is again *Incarnation* - we eat and drink bread and wine said to be the body and blood of God - because we are in some strange way the body and blood of God ourselves (humans filled with deity). Thus again it *makes true what already is.* The more I think about it the more the whole Christian story is about making true what already is.

Christ comes to show humans who they are, not what they are not. The sacrificial love displayed on the cross does not change God's mind about us (as the so called objective views of the Atonement).[34] The spectacle of the cross changes us not God! How? By displaying costly love rather than brutal judgement.

If we see Jesus as a literal, perfect offering, a human blood sacrifice, then we have no choice but to view God as wrathful, and who needs his mind changing by having Jesus pay the price for our sins. He dies, we get let off the hook! But if we see the symbol of the god-man Jesus hanging on a tree as a selfless act of love, joining humankind at its ugliest, lowest, shittiest place, and not retaliating with any sense of hatred or revenge, then there is more chance of our own view of God being changed. We might even fall in love with such a loving God rather than being terrified of Him. Thus the Jesus-Tree can either perpetuate a Toxic view of God or it can heal it.

Increasingly I see the human family as, at its core, somehow strangely divine, and the church's role as being about awakening folk to their hidden inner divinity rather than 'converting them to a new religion'. This is the role, not just of the Church, but nature based / pagan religions too. Centuries before Jesus the multitude of god-man myths (that we find in Egypt, Greece, Persia and all over the ancient world) were there to point to the belief that all were sons and daughters of the gods. I've naturally started to see the whole of creation as buzzing with life, energy and deity. A few years ago I was interviewed for a radio show and the interviewer asked me where I most experience the presence of God. Without a moment's hesitation I said, 'within the forest', and went on to describe the local forest as 'My Natural Cathedral'.

I am a dreamer, and have in the past found it very difficult to actually notice beauty all around me. Put me in a gallery of paintings and I will usually start to read *into* the artwork before actually seeing it for what it is. The same has been true for a garden full of flowers, or even streets full of people. The expression 'can't see the wood for the trees' comes to mind. I might seem ignorant when I walk straight past someone in the street, but the truth is I didn't see her. I was too busy imagining some great voyage or dreaming of the next book to write.

In my first book I talk about 'looking without seeing'. It is one of the most basic roles of meditation - to help folk to wake up to the present and stop dreaming about the past or the future.

I'm truly delighted that, though still a dreamer, I'm now beginning to spend more and more time in the present, and can actually now look and *see*. I often take our family dog for walks up the forest and, every time, I am truly blown away by the beauty of the sights, sounds and smells up there. I find the forest a deeply inspiring place to sit and ponder. I still allow my imaginative side to play but I also notice things that I would have once missed, like the feeling of the leaves brushing across my face, or the tiny spider crafting her intricate web in the hollowed out area of a branch.

The following is a journal entry of a recent forest walk. I was literally over-awed by the power of nature:

*'As I stepped out of the car into the rich green surroundings of the forest I experienced something quite profound. I was suddenly*

*struck by a natural orchestra of sound. Nature's spring time musicians played their instruments and the whole area was an amphitheatre of exquisite song. I wish I knew all the names of the various singers... I could make out a few: the tweets of the various tits, the caw of the crow, the occasional quoo quoo of the dove, some distant others closer, all held together by the skillful invisible baton held by Mother Nature herself. The experience was breathtaking.'*

Such is the power of the forest for me I now find it my main place of inspiration for writing. It's also where I met a *real* Wizard.

Chapter 9

# Meeting Merlin

*Raven carried her ball of light into the sky,*
*So we no longer live in darkness.*
   *The old self image must die*
*Death must precede the*
*Psychological revolution that is welling*
*The creative reorganization demanding to*
*Unblock the flow of psychic energy and*
*Give life new meaning*
   *Into the cauldron Raven*
*Beautiful soul maiden gently places*
*Black seeds from my shadow*
*Black wormseed from my ego*
*To incubate, regenerate and*
*Facilitate rebirth*
   *A beginning, the end*
*Dying to the senses, withdrawing*
*Voluntarily entering the dark inner world of the soul*
*At home in the darkness of suffering*
*Only in death is a greater thing born*
*Only within the darkness lie germs of recovery*
Heather Blakey[35]

What could be more wonderful than a life of sharing your most magical experiences and deepest longings with the world? What could be more satisfying than a daily workout at the PC, where you allow your creative inner voice to make meaning out of all the mess and muddle of life? What could be more therapeutic than to be still and *listen* to the (usually silent) 'wiser you' as he or she gently whispers in your ear?

For me writing is a natural and necessary part of who I am. I do not consider myself to be particularly *good*, but am most definitely passionate and committed. I write because it is the place where *I* can talk to *myself*. I write because I am always chattering inside my head, and the computer keyboard is the gymnasium through which I can release some of that mental activity. I write because I have discovered that the often confused arguments within are miraculously sifted and sorted as they eventually find their way from my brain, through my fingers, to the screen in front of my eyes. I see the full print-out tray as the first destination of a recycled piece of garbage that began its journey among countless other bits of plastic and waste, having been organised, modified and purified along the way. And that's only the beginning, for then it sets out on the next stage of the voyage, where it is inspected in fine detail, melted down, re-formed and re-packaged for the retail shelves. This we call the publishing process.

In the introduction I mentioned my first book, *The Gospel of Falling Down*. It's a book I wrote whilst preparing for a three day retreat I'd been asked to lead by my good friend James Fahey of the then Winford Manor Retreat House.[36] I came up with the idea of leading three days on the theme of human failure and how to look at our bumps, bruises and brokenness creatively. I decided to use illusions and visual tricks as metaphorical object lessons for the sessions. I wanted the attendees to be somehow re-enchanted and plugged back in to the deep feelings of magic and wonder they would have had as children yet probably rarely experienced as adults. I used personal stories, magical effects, myths and spiritual exercises to enable the participants to look deeply into the flaws and cracks of their lives and find the beauty within them, the hidden gold, the glittering diamond that sparkles inside us all.

It worked well and gave me the necessary confidence to want

to take my ideas further. In fact I'd stumbled across something that has become a hallmark of my ministry - the combination of the brokenness theme and the experience of magic. I learned from this that we writers should always use who we are and what we believe to say what we say. I am passionate about magic and I am passionate about enabling people to live with (and even love) their imperfections. I let this passion flow into my writing which makes it feel genuine and accessible. Any passion and any interest can be used in this way.

So, ironically my retreat on failure turned out to be a success. I still regularly run it. One of the main exercises I use enables participants to learn how to contact and listen to their own voice of inner wisdom (something we all have). Part of my preparation for the Retreat involved me re-reading my entire spiritual journal to see how much my religious understanding had changed over the years, but as I read it something shocked me. There was a very hurt, angry and often downright whining voice within my writings, and it was *my* voice. The voice was extremely self-critical, negative and defensive. It was as if I thought the whole world was against me. There were huge chunks of self-flagellation: *"Oh God why am I such an x, y, z."* And, *"Why do people hate me so much?"* There were also little rituals of repentance where I promised God, yet again not to re-start smoking etc. (This voice has probably not been altogether absent from the book you are now holding).

A few days later I decided to read it again and this time something else leapt out. There was *another voice* within the writings, a more grown up and peaceful voice. I had accidentally stumbled across what spiritual teachers and psychologists have been teaching for years; the fact that we all have a deeper, wiser and more mature voice within our consciousness. It's just that we usually play out our life scenarios through the more shallow and immature self of the ego. As I read on I saw how this wiser self almost answered the brattish questions and complaints of the whining self. I now call these two voices the 'little-me' and the 'divine-me'. The little-me, so I claim in *Falling Down*, is what some spiritual traditions and psychological schools call the ego, the false-self, or the imperial I. Whereas the divine-me corresponds to what Jungian psychology calls *the* Self. Others might call it the God-Self, or simply The Essence. What I found astonishing, when re-reading my journal, was that it seemed to be written by two different people, one of them calmly answering the defensive and sulky little outbursts of the other. It was like a discussion between a client and a counsellor, the latter gently offering words of wisdom to a soul in need. The fact that I had let out so much anguish, via the little-me, had led to some beautiful breakthroughs, where my anger and rage had literally turned into wisdom.

The truth I'd stumbled across lies somewhere at the heart of all great spirituality, from Zen to The Twelve Steps.[37] When we come to the end of our own resources and feel like giving up altogether, we are (ironically) closer to the breakthrough than we would have been without it. It is the pivotal place of immense possibility. It is where the cracks and flaws can expose us to the beauty of our deep inner treasures. It is what Zen calls the beginner's mind, Franciscans call poverty, St. Paul calls weakness, recovering alcoholics call powerlessness, Carmelites call Nada (nothingness), Buddhists call emptiness and Genesis calls nakedness etc. When we come to this place we are most stripped of our (manufactured) selves and yet most open to our (true) selves.

What follows is an extract from *Falling Down* which is an example of all that has just been said. I was sat in front of my computer feeling like shit, not knowing what to do or where to go. At that point in my life I was seeing a therapist and taking antidepressants. Certain people in my parish were being brutish, threats were coming from elsewhere, and I felt like I had no one to turn to. All I really wanted was to be a good priest.

For some reason I started typing and it became a spontaneous conversation between me and myself - the pitiful whining me (what I call the little-me) and some other part of me that I still feel slightly in awe of (my true Self perhaps?). The wiser / calmer voice said much more than he usually does on this occasion. Perhaps it was because the deeper me knew just how much I was at rock bottom and needed a great deal of help. It comes across as a dialogue between me and God and, bearing in mind when it was written, does use a lot of biblical imagery [I'm afraid that's just how it came out]. Even so, it contains a fully universal message. When reading it, try to see it as a conversation between my two inner voices.

Rock bottom is an illuminating term for you can't fall further than the hitting of that rock. It is there that the fall breaks. But there is something else too. A rock is solid ground. A rock will not collapse. A rock is a place on which you can actually build. I find that an amazing thought, we cannot build in thin air, yet so many of us try. We can only truly build from the solid and honest place of the rock at the bottom – the place where *we are who we are*.

*'I want to die. Everything's lost. I can't believe I've been so stupid and let my guard down. God, I am a waste of time, a pathetic little shit who just can't do anything right. Why the hell do you bother with me?'*

**'Keep talking Mark'.**

*'I just wanted to do it right God, I wanted to have what other people have, what other clergy have, a little bit of respect! Why don't people trust me? I'm not a threat to anyone. Why do they seem to despise me so much? Why do those people keep making me feel like I'll never be good enough for them? All I can see now is bloody darkness. Who the hell am I God?'*

**'You are Mark and I love you'.**

*'But who is Mark?'*

**'Mark is simply the name your parents gave you. But your**

*problem is that you confuse the Mark that you want to be (and try so hard to be) with the one who you already are. Now if you really want me to answer your question, 'But who is Mark?' then allow me to lead you somewhere in your imagination and trust me.*

'I'll try.'

*'No, too much trying is your problem Mark. For once let go of your controlling nature and allow yourself to be taken on a journey. All you need to be is open.*

*Mark, I am going to take you to a place that you may have heard about, but you might not recognise. I am going to take you to meet yourself. Just let me lead your thoughts...*

*You are falling... you are falling into a dark abyss.'*

'I'm already there.'

*'Don't talk Mark, just let me lead your thoughts. As you fall you see the clothes you've been wearing begin to split and tear at the seams. Your priest's clothing is in tatters, the beautiful vestments are now rags. But you notice that there are other clothes now appearing on your body in their place. You can see the academic gown and colourful university hood you wore when you sat with your proud family to receive your degree. But now they are ripped and shredded and flung off into space.*

*As you keep falling more and more clothes appear, and are then in tatters. Clothes from work, combats from the Royal Marine selection weekend, school and scout uniforms, and all the clothes you wore as you went through all those fashion fads, like punk rock bondage suits, teddy boy style drapes and drainpipes, hippy afghan coats still smelling of patchouli, and the various costumes from all the martial arts clubs you've belonged to. They are all now in fragments as you are left still falling and totally naked.*

*Suddenly there is a thud as your fall is broken. You manage to stand up and look at yourself – battered, bruised and nude. You feel more vulnerable than ever before and try to work out who on earth you are for you cannot seem to remember anything. All the things you have ever done are now just a distant memory. All those* achievements, experiences, and interests that have given you your identity are no more. You try to grasp at some of the labels you've applied to yourself but nothing comes. You feel frightened, disorientated and alone.'

*'Oh God this is not helping'*

'Quiet Mark, and trust me. Come back to the imaginative exercise. Because of the emotional intensity of the falling experience you feel exhausted and lie down. Before you know it you are asleep. Watch yourself sleeping Mark. Look at how peaceful your sleep is. You have just been through an experience like nothing before, but you have no bad memories to keep your mind buzzing. For once your over active mind is still. You are sleeping like a baby. Now watch yourself wake up. You rise and discover yourself in a beautiful garden. The sleep has been good for you, but because of the stripping away of all your labels and layers you don't really know who you are.'

*'Oh God stop now, this is NOT helping. I asked you to show me who I am, not make me more confused by conjuring up imaginative fantasies about my amnesia'.*

'You will soon discover who you are Mark, just trust and be led. You walk past a gorgeous tree full of the most exquisite fruit you've ever seen before, and you notice a little pathway, which you decide to follow. You walk on a hundred yards or so to a lovely pond, and you can see fish swimming near the surface that seem to have golden coloured backs. You peer in to take a closer look and can see you own refection. It is you but a 'you' that you have never seen before. You seem so alive, and though you know the fish are gold coloured you distinctly see the glimmer of gold in your own reflection. You can't help but smile and your smile brightens the whole of the surface of the pond.

Then you stop, for across the pond you catch a glimpse of someone else. As you look at her she seems familiar but you can't place her. Is it your mother that she reminds you of, or your sister, or your daughter, or is it that woman from the superstore who served you last weekend? You look again and the crazy thing is that she reminds you of all of them… in fact of every woman and girl you know. And then she calls out to you, 'Hello Adam'.

'Who? Why the hell did she call me Adam?'

'Not hell Mark, but heaven, for this is how it was before hell was let loose inside the human mind.

Mark, this is who you truly are. Adam – before the fall – is your inner self. Adam is every man, and Eve is every woman. Their story is your story. Their sin was not stealing fruit but wanting to become what they were not. Mark, I have created a mechanism for coming back to who you truly are. Adam fell from grace, but your falls can be into grace if you allow them to be.'

'Oh God, are you telling me that when I fall, and can no longer rely on my labels, that I can become like Adam and Eve, before they were cast out of the garden?'

'Adam and Eve still exist Mark. They exist within all people, and they still live outside the garden. You live outside Eden. I tried to bring you all back into the garden when I came as the Second Adam, but you misunderstood my teaching and built another system that keeps people separate from me. Mark there is a way back to the garden – where you will see your inner gold – and it is to simply trust in me. Trust me when I say that I love you as you are. Do you realise, Mark, that you only fall because you need to fall? And you only need to fall because you always want to run away from your true self. You are obsessed with climbing up to where you think you should be. The falling is simply the way everything corrects itself.

'I still don't get this. I hate falling. It hurts and makes me feel like dying. I want to be well thought of, special, loved and valued. I try to be what I try to be because I am not content with the shit that I am. I want to achieve. I want to be a good priest. I want to feel respected. I want to be loved.'

'And you will never achieve any of those dreams if you keep on avoiding who you really are by climbing that ladder. Mark, listen to *this: you cannot achieve these things because you already have them. You are already loved by a force greater than anything. You are special Mark, as is every other person who lives. And if you stayed for longer in the place where you can see how special you are, then the changes you so deserve will come about naturally, rather than in a manufactured way.*

*Look once more Mark, at that person by the side of the pond in the garden. It IS you. He is the you that I created and who still exists inside and under all those layers of your complicated personality. You will never remove all those layers, nor should you try, for they have brought great lessons of their own. But when you do fall again, remember to look out for the one with the golden smile – HE IS THERE AND HE IS YOU. And my dream for you Mark, is that as time goes on you will need less falls, and will be able to spend longer with the gold.'* [38]

More recently I have discovered that we don't just have two inner voices. We have many of them, all of which add together to make up our very complex personalities. One of them, however, lies deep down beneath the others. It is the true Self (what I call the divine-me). This is what I refer to in my second book as the wizard within. It is precisely the divine-me or wizard within that I now hope to be open to when I write. But we can't force it to happen. We can't manufacture it. It is simply as if the very act of writing unlocks and enables this voice to be heard. Sometimes the wisdom this voice imparts is quite breathtaking, to the point of being quasi-psychic.

I didn't realise when I was writing it but *The Wizard's Gift* was a story I wrote for myself in the future! Every time I pick it up now I see something else, little lessons that help me cope with what's going in my life. What's odd is that those lessons could not have been understood back when I wrote them, for the experiences they describe had not occurred then. It is a short novel that continues the theme of listening to the inner voice but in the form of an adult fairy tale. It is of course primarily a story written for whoever decides to read it but I am amazed and delighted by how it speaks to my current situation. I am also amazed by how it articulates what I have since discovered is a naturally Druidic spirituality.

The book's central character is a young suicidal man called Sam. He has been completely screwed up by years of indoctrination from a strict cult-like religious group. He flees to a forest with a mission: to take his own life. However he escapes his attempt at self-destruction and eventually meets a wise old man deep in the heart of the forest. The old man becomes a Merlin-like figure to Sam, and through this wizard's gentle advice and special gifts, he unlocks many secrets about his own personality... the final one revealing his real identity for the very first time – he gets to meet his true self. The book is also something of a bridge between the Christian and Pagan worlds - an attempt to make some connections between the two [I wrote it while I was still a vicar].

The bare bones of the book were written in that very forest at a place called 'The Reading Place'. In my novel I call it The Reading Chair. It is a lovely pagan-looking circular bench where folk can stop for a quiet moment's reflection. It was created by the wonderful Carver and Coppersmith, Richard Taylor.

The inspiration for The Wizard's Gift came while I was walking my dog. I started imagining myself walking alongside a wise old man. My imagination ran wild as I began to hear him giving me all sorts of advice for living etc. Immediately I knew I had another book.

All my books are evidence that a pretty messed up and highly imperfect guy can, with a little bit of self-belief and a whole lot of passion, see his dreams come to reality. I am convinced that everyone can write and that everyone can be inspired. We all have he inner guide. He / she is there waiting to be discovered. Trust me there is a wise wizard within us all.

*Be still!*

*Listen!*

*Can you hear him?*

*Stop for a moment… close your eyes… be here NOW!*

*Are you aware?*

*There is a forest… an ancient wood… a scary sacred place in you.*

*It can seem like an overgrown jungle of thoughts - densely compacted trees and bushes smothered in twisted vines and creepers.*

*These are the intertwined confusions of memories, assumptions, fears, beliefs, prejudices, judgements, failures and successes.*

*They are the many layers of ego clothing we've dressed in over the years. They form the background noise of our mind. Sometimes they are quieter, but sometimes they deafen us, ruling out any clarity of vision.*

*Stop!*

*Be still!*

*Be here NOW!*

*Notice the voices blowing like wind through the trees…*

*Be aware of the echoes of arguments, unfinished plans, inner dialogues of confusion, and the incessant demands of the inner citric.*

*Notice them and the notice that you are noticing them.*

*See, they are NOT you. They are just remnants of past experiences and dreams of future hopes…*

*Be still!*

*Be here NOW where neither past nor future exist and then you will be ready to meet him.*

*Meet who?*

*There is an inhabitant within this scary sacred wood - a dweller who is real. Someone lives here whose presence transforms it from a frightening jungle to an enchanted forest.*

*He is quiet… he waits for you to stop and come to him.*

*He is not forceful.*

*He stands with lamp in hand, there in the deepest, darkest heart of the forest.*

*He is the wise One…*

*The true inner guide...*
*The divine voice...*
*The higher Self...*
*He is the Wizard Within.*[39]

# Chapter 10

# The Wizard Speaks Again!

*I feel the raven behind me move forwards into my body; I sense her warm down feathers and rib bones, then her wings half open briefly as she settles, and I feel the strength of her shoulders, broad and pushing slightly forwards. I relax, accepting, finding the way that we fit, and she rises up into my face, looking through my eyes at the gathering. She feels so dispassionate compared with the vulnerability of the aching me beneath human skin. I relax, exhaling once again, and as her consciousness touches mine, her visions flow into my mind.*
Emma Restall Orr [40]

I like to spend as much time as I can in the forest because it hums with the magic of nature. This 'natural magic' exists all around us and within us. Externally it is the pulse, the throb, the beating heart of the planet, the flowing energy of all things. This is why forests are so sacred to nature-based paths like Druidry. It's also why they are like great cathedrals to me.

Internally there are various manifestations of this natural magic, one of which is what I've previously referred to as the wizard within. We all have an inner guide, a magician, living deep down inside us. We each have an ability to create wonders, to heal our hurting psyches and sometimes even to conjure up the necessary energy to achieve things that are seemingly impossible. Often this voice is heard when we've come to the very end of our own strength, to the limit of our own resources. One such experience came to me on September 30th 2008. It had been a particularly difficult few weeks. Life had been hard (at times unbearable) and the forest was the only place I felt I could turn.

The almost daily traumas of the past year since leaving the church, had left a huge heaviness hanging over my wife and I. The *only* regret I do have about my decision of May 2007 was that my poor wife has ended up paying as much for my mistakes as me. I thought everything was coming crumbling to an end.

I sought out the Reading Chair, the place where my invented character Sam had met the Wizard so many times. I sat down, opened my journal, and started to write:

*Having just walked up through the glorious corridor of trees and been once more enchanted by the living, breathing, chlorophyll green cathedral, I now sit at my favourite spot - the Reading Chair. Here is where I first met the Wizard. Here is where I was given the Wizard's Gift. It's raining and the green surroundings are pulsing with life, colour and richness. But inside I am wounded.*

[Just as I had written the above words I heard a deep and guttural honk coming from above, and to my surprise and delight saw her as she flew overhead, a raven. How majestic, how rare and how perfect. I continued]

*This is a truly strange situation. I am at the same time both enchanted and wounded. I am sitting with deep emotional pain. Things have been so difficult ever since our honeymoon last year. The pressure on my wife and I has been unbelievable, and quite unbearable. I'm so scared I'm going to lose her. And it's so hard living in my head. The constant churning of negative thoughts is quite exhausting. The Enneagram[41] personality test labels me a tragic romantic. How true that is. Ironically, this is the place where my Sam nearly ended it all.[42] Well I'm not quite that desperate but it does feel like another kind of death. My poor wife. My decision has altered our lives so drastically, and it has been particularly hard for her. The pent up emotional intensity for us both has been so draining, no one to let it out to, nobody to talk it through with. And outward anger often turned inward, to ourselves and to each other.*

[Then, as so often happens, my words changed from being a first person diary style entry to a second person voice to myself]

*'Little brother... look around you... look at all the life... look at the apples on those trees over there. They are red and rich and full of blessing. And look on the floor beneath the trees. See the fallen, broken, bruised and rotting apples. Yet these damaged apples are also full of blessing and life giving potential. They are now food for the many creatures that live on the ground, and they are nourishment for your mother the earth herself. Look Mark... take it all in... what you see is nature's way... a constant recycling of all things. And not just a recycling but a transfiguration of rottenness and ugliness too.*

*And listen. What can you hear? The wind whistling through the trees; the countless birds chirping, squawking and chattering. Mark you are where you are meant to be. Your own fallen-ness and cracked shell has now led you to a place of re-birth. Inside you still feel frightened, winded, sick and sad, but all this will be transformed if you can but learn to trust in the will of the universe. Use what you have to bring blessing and nourishment to others. Stop feeling so ashamed of the past, it's over now. Today is here. Live in it. Love your life and love all you have but without futile demands. Do this and all will be well.*

*And look once again, Mark. But look deeper, at a psychic level. Open your intuitive eyes and see what's here. The forest is alive with friends, friends for you. I am inside you and I am alive in everything you see. I am energies, gods, spirits, fairies. I live under every stone, within every leaf, in the living and dying polarities of nature. I am the sun behind the clouds, I am the sweet droplets of rain on your neck. I am the connectedness of it all. I am your Raven Spirit who guides you. Learn to look, see the lessons Mother Nature has. Look for synchronicities. Look for guidance. It all has a message. It's speaking, constantly. See it and celebrate it, this is your new calling. Interpret the signs and make meaning for self and others. Believe. All will be well.'*

*Then, as if Mother Nature added her own full stop to all that had been said I looked up and an apple fell right in front of me. A sign - a fallen apple. I will let my own fallen and bruised apples bring life now.*

I am getting more used to this kind of magic, inspired by more time spent with nature. Another similar encounter occurred a few weeks later. I was sat at a wedding fair, in the beautiful surroundings of my friend's North Somerset mansion, Winford Manor. There was a moment of quiet and I decided to take out a pen and sheet of paper and look for inspiration for my book. Suddenly I found myself writing this:

*How do I express the most difficult parts of my story? How do I keep it honest and true yet also continue to talk only of my own errors and not those of others who've crossed my path?*

[Almost immediately an answer came, which I scribbled down. Then I looked at what I'd written]

**Little brother, human life is messy, imperfect, shady. There is a shadow every time the sun shines down upon you, simultaneously enabling your god-self to glow and yet your shadow to be even more obvious. Do not fight the shadow. Rather look into it and trust that it, too, has a message for you. The work of alchemy is not just about transforming lead into gold but to show that you are lead and gold and both are part of the glory.**

**Little brother you bravely took the painful consequence for past errors. Let them now begin to transform you. Walk with me little brother, come to the stone circle. I have a lesson for you...**

[Well, of course I gathered my pen and pad and made my way down to the wonderful circle of twelve stones situated in the orchard of Winford Manor. I sat down just inside the circumference, where bonfires are made and stories told into the night. I was awestruck and full of anticipation, waiting for the story my inner self was about to tell me. *This is exactly what happened.* I knew the place quite well but not in any great detail. A dreamer (like me) looks but doesn't really see. But that day I started to see things that totally amazed me. Not only was I sat inside a circle of 12 rocks, I was also sat inside a triangle of three great trees... three huge sweet chestnuts]

*There, now relax and look at the tree in front of you Mark... what do you see?*

*I see an ancient looking tree, clearly the oldest of the three in this triangle... it has a trunk as a wide as a small car.*

**Little Brother this tree is strong, rooted and ancient. It contains wisdom in its branches. Look. See how new, fresh, green sprigs burst out from its trunk and branches. It is your future – this tree – it is a glimpse of a future you, moulded by the hallmarks of life – the knocks, the sawn off branches, the pruning away of old dead material, the badly weathered and damaged places... it is the great protective wise guide – your older self.**

**Now look behind you Mark. (I turned round) What do you see?**

*I see a tree that is clearly the middle-aged one of the trinity.*

**This one is you now – smaller, yet still strong, rooted and able to grow fresh green twigs. But it's the youngest one over there that will really interest you. Look at it. Can you see your twisted past? Can you see the face?**

*I can. I can see a twisted and complicated tree with a distinctive human face-like feature on the right hand side.*

**The face in that tree is turned away. He cannot bear to look at you – he is ashamed. He is your wounded self of the past. This tree has the least amount of fresh greenery growing from it, yet it is the**

*youngest and ought to be the healthiest. The trees of the present and the future bear more fruit little brother.*

[I walked over to the youngest tree and, as I did so, the face gradually disappeared. I then stood under it and gazed up into the branches... then and down at the ground]

*It's amazing... there are more spiky chestnut shells here than under the other two trees. Yet there is not so much green life on the actual branches. This one, though seemingly in poorer shape, has more fruit than the other two.*

**Mark, little brother, pick one of them up... and keep it as a symbol of the recovered fruit of your own rejected past. Face the past and your guilty face disappears. Face the past and recover the fruit – nothing is wasted.**

**Now go sit once more inside the stone circle.**

[I walked back, sat down again, and faced the tree of the present – the middle aged-tree]

**Little brother, see the shape that its double trunk and branches are making. It creates a triangular doorway... a triangle within a triangle. The present is now a doorway into a new experience. Liberated from the past, and at peace with the future, you are free to live in the present.**

**Little brother, do not doubt your self any more. You have suffered enough from consequences of past failures. Now live, learn, give, love, laugh, make merry, be free, be you.**

*Thank you my wizard... my good teacher.*

When I got home I searched the internet for the symbolic meaning of chestnut trees. What I discovered was awesome:

I learned how the 12$^{th}$ Century Christian mystic Hildegard von Bingen praised the chestnut for its ability to make natural remedies for the prolonging of life. Also Celtic druids apparently made handles and staffs out of chestnut because they believed touching these was a way to draw out energies of longevity and invigoration.

Because Chestnuts drop in the fall they have been regarded as a symbol of harvest, abundance and preparation, thus including a message that now is the time to gather and rejoice in the gifts we have.

Chestnuts have been seen as symbolic of *honesty, opportunity and wisdom* and have been associated with the following professions: Teachers, lecturers, researchers, trainers and priests.

# Chapter 11

# The Three Magics – 3

*If you have chosen Raven, magic is in the air. Do not try to figure it out; you cannot.*

*It is the power of the unknown at work, and something special is about to happen.*

*The deeper mystery, however, is how you will respond to the sparkling*

*Synchronicity of this alchemical moment. Will you recognize it*

*And use it to further enhance your growth?*

Medicine Cards[43]

Journal notes:

*I can see my magic changing yet again. It is as if my performance magic is at last becoming ONE with what some refer to as 'real magic'.*

Ten years ago I used magic as an illustrative tool. I was nervous of giving it any more status than that for the reasons previously stated. Then a few years into my second post (while still using a disclaimer) my magic naturally took on a more mysterious feel and became less a tool for object lessons and more an art form to evoke wonder and enchantment. However over the last few years my understanding of magic has evolved still further, to the point where I now see stage (deceptive) magic as having the power to awaken us to real magic.

This tradition goes back many thousands of years to the earliest shamanic practises of ancient native cultures. As Eugene Burger and Robert Neale conclude in their masterpiece *Magic and*

*Meaning*, magical trickery has been used all over the world by the medicine or holy men of various traditional cultures. With reference to shamanic healing rituals Eugene Burger says, 'The shaman's deception may in this sense, be the necessary lie that brings others to trust in healing powers – and, thereby contributes toward bringing about the healing experience.'[44] This is not saying that these rituals are 'a con.' They are totally different from the approach of modern day charlatans who use deception alone to make people believe in a form of magic that they themselves do not actually believe in (and who's clients are then willing to hand over vast amounts of money). Such fraud-sters have been found in all places, from theatrical medium shows to evangelical healing crusades, but their discovery does not mean that such magic cannot happen. As a magician (illusionist) I know how easy it is to convince folk of special powers, but just because that's true I would never dare suggest that special powers do not therefore exist.

In the case of the ancient shamans their use of magical trickery is not fraud but a powerful placebo to evoke the possibility of real magic (healing) to take place. The big difference in this and the cheap con-men who rip off the vulnerable is that the shaman does believe in the real power of the magic. As Eugene Burger says:

> '*consider the well-discussed case of the shaman sucking an illness from a patient and then spitting up a worm (or other object) that was previously concealed in the shaman's hand or mouth. One might see the expelled worm as a material symbol of the spirit-world reality. Since both shaman and patient believe that it is the intrusion into the body of physical objects that causes the illness in the first place, the shaman must therefore convince the patient that the illness causing object has been removed.*'[45]

It seems to me that life is essentially magical and that, far from being supernatural, magic is very natural. As science advances, more and more of what we once saw as magic is able to be explained and understood. Of course I'm not talking about flying around on magic carpets or having fights with Harry Potter wands that can shoot lightening bolts. This is symbolic magic which points to the deeper natural magic. When you see David Copperfield float over an audience without any wires, or when you watch a movie about a lazy young sorcerer who makes a broomstick clean a magical laboratory or, for that matter, when you see a white bearded Charlton Heston raise his staff over the red sea and the waters part in the name of Jehovah, this is all symbolic magic that points to the deeper natural magic of life.

Clearly my departure from the establishment of the church's ministry has released my magical gift and allowed it to take on a new significance. I find this marvellous because I was afraid the reverse would happen, that my magic would suffer as a result of leaving the ministry. This is something I wrote in my journal as I was pondering my magic and its development:

'I realized something wonderful today. For years I thought that if I ever left the church's ministry my magic would somehow suffer and become mere secular entertainment – void of any spiritual depth or heart. However the reverse it true. Since leaving the church my magic has taken on an even richer spiritual dimension. Performing magic has become my new vocation. I am a priest of magic! I am beginning to realize that all magic effects are real magic – because they point us to that magical world that lies behind and beyond all things. To watch a magic effect opens a window inside our imaginations, through which (if we trust the experience) we are privileged to climb and play for a while.

I've already mentioned how psychological theories teach us that we have a left and right brain hemisphere, the right-brain being the source of our more intuitive, poetic and mystical (psychic) impulses, and the left-brain being the source of all that is rational, analytical, literal and theoretical.[46] Various things (not least the expectations of our rationalistic society) go together to make many (perhaps even most western) adults much more left-brain orientated than right. This leaves us in a state where genuine adventures into the realm of wonder and enchantment become a mere childhood memory. In my experience magic cracks open the left-brain and evokes a state of openness and child-like awe. Now I push this even further and believe that magic (as illusion) opens us to the possibility of a deeper magical consciousness.

While writing the above words my inbox bleeped to let me know an email had arrived. It was from my good friend and fellow magician Rob Chapman. As I stopped writing to reply to his message I also mentioned that I was working on notions of the interrelationship between stage magic and real magic. Rob is not only an excellent stage magician but also a Druid Grade member of OBOD. He co-leads a Druidic community with his lovely partner Wendy. I should have known he'd see my email as a challenge. This is what turned up in my inbox a few minutes later:

'How does performance magic connect with real magic? Ooooeeerrr there's a small thought for the day. The way I see it is that real magic is not about something happening or disappearing. It is a set of occurrences that just for a moment - when they all come together - bring our awareness into full reality, the world - just for an instant - stops and we get the sense that we are very much a part of the bigger picture. This can happen in ritual, in meditation or it can happen in a smile that just reaches in and connects us. In that moment, nothing matters, in that moment there is just The Moment. As stage magicians we have a choice, we can be the trickster, the guy on the corner, exciting people with the thrill of the chase, or we can be the mystic / the wizard etc. We can choose to create, hopefully moments when our audience feels the world stop, and all that exists is a moment of wonder. In that way we are no different, except maybe we try to consciously create those moments for others and ourselves rather than hoping that they may happen. Our rituals are the prayers and blessings we offer to spirit before a performance asking the divine mystery to flow through us and use us to connect people to all that is magical. Our altar is the table, our ritual tools our props, I know that for me now I feel the same connection in prepping for a gig as I do for getting ready for a ritual. We bring the sacred out, the mystery of the moment. In which case there is no difference, other than method, each a journey to the same end.' Rob

Those words sent shivers down my spine as I sat at my computer screen taking them in. It is great to know Rob, not least because so many (performance) magicians tend to be sceptics. On the one hand that's not really surprising because every stage magician knows the long (and shady) history of how various unscrupulous individuals have used conjuring-type techniques to con poor unsuspecting people out of money, in return for a 'real' glimpse into the supernatural. The Magic Circle has an official Board whose purpose is to check out and (if necessary) expose such individuals. Over the last few decades some very well known stage psychics have been caught using trickery. Do a Google-search 'frauds in the spiritual world' and you'll even come up with names of a few Christian ministers who've resorted to the same techniques, and claimed their powers as 'words of knowledge' or 'prophetic gifts from God'.

I've been to lectures by magicians who, in their passion to rid the world of such con-men, teach audiences the art of cold reading[47] which they seem to assume every tarot reader and astrologer in the country uses. They don't. I've met many and have not yet come across one who uses cold reading. I've also read hundreds of divinatory books and, again, have not come across any that advocate cold reading.

My wife and I find it amusing that, when we first met, she was the psychically open-minded one and I was the sceptic.

Three years later and the roles have been almost fully reversed. While Jodie has developed a healthy criticism of the world of mediums, and even a deep dislike of the world of religion, I have had to eat my previously sceptical words time and time again. It's as if a new magical awareness is dawning in my psyche.

Of course, I'm still aware that frauds do exist and that mind readers and mentalists could easily convince folk they're for real. Yet I have come across more and more people who just seem to be 'naturally magical'. I've even had the experience of my own magic (tricks) seemingly cross the border into being more than just tricks. The synchronicities that occur within my performance are sometimes astonishing. I know mere coincidences happen, but the amount of times I now stop having to do actual tricks and sit back to simply allow magic to happen without my intervention is quite breath-taking.

Two things are happening to me this side of the 'magic doorway', the magic is working it's own magic on me - drawing me deeper into a more right-brain world, and the druidic and nature based experiences are making everything seem more alive and more magical. It is as if I am actually experiencing within myself what I've been talking about and enabling others to experience for years. The universe is becoming an enchanted space again. I am beginning to believe again – to believe in things that I'd long assigned to the garage bin of childhood fantasy.

As Thomas More, the one time Catholic monk and author of the best seller Care of the Soul, says:

'When I was a child in school, I would sit at my desk half listening to the teacher telling us how many square miles made up the state of Michigan and how to do compound interest. My mind was occupied with far more serious issues: Do dragons exist? Was there ever a Flood? Were Adam and Eve real?

It took me years of education, a Ph.D. in religion, and then more years of independent reading and writing before I felt I had answers to my pressing questions. I passed through a period where I was convinced through elaborate theories of metaphor and psychological projection that fairies and dragons were symbols and metaphors, or were real in fantasy only. For a long time, I believed in Jung's unconscious and considered it a good explanation for such things. But now, finally, I've come to realize that dragons are real, fairies do indeed dance, and the Flood of the Bible is more real than the flooding on the evening news.'[48]

So what I recognise as the third stage of my magic's evolution is this magic that awakens us to *real* magic.

Before I close this chapter I want to talk about something I'm rapidly discovering about the modern Druidic understanding of magic. In fact Druidry is so difficult to put into a box [one of the reasons I love it] that there are clearly many different Druidic notions of magic. However, I have noticed a common theme among Druid authors, and it is a theme that has made great sense to me, even tying in with my Christian past and the notion of prayer.

Whereas many forms of paganism believe in and openly practise the magic of rituals, prayers and spells to cause actual change, it is very hard to find Druidic books on ritual magic or spellcraft. You can find them if you look hard enough, but even when you do there seems to be a more cautious approach. For many modern Druids magic is what life is – and to be fully immersed or plugged in to the flowing energy of life on this enchanted planet is how living a magical life is understood. It is less to do with forcing actual changes to take place and more about soaking up the magic of what already is. So the magic of transformation is about the transforming of the person needing the magic, rather than his or her material situation. What is often needed is not a new situation but a new way of perceiving it.

This is where it ties in with Christian prayer: Is petitionary prayer to do with transforming a situation and solving a problem by changing actual circumstances or is it more to do with changing the praying person's perspective? It's possibly a 'both and', but I tend towards the latter. I feel that to pray through a difficult problem helps the praying person come to his or her own conclusions about how to deal with the problem. The actual problem will rarely go away but a new way of looking at it might relieve the power of the problem in that person's life.

I'm not saying that prayers for actual change are in any way unnatural – such compulsions are very natural, and sometimes 'miracles' do seem to occur, but in my experience the prayer of surrender to a situation often yields a more healthy result than to try and force change which, when it refuses to come, causes just more misery. It is the difference between saying that through prayer or magic 'you can *have* what you *want*', or through prayer or magic 'you can learn to *want* what you *have*'.

With reference to 'supernatural' magic I've actually come across many Druid authors who say they do not believe in supernatural magic because magic is simply *part* of nature – magic is therefore totally natural. And with reference to spellcraft there is a healthy respect among Druid authors (and other paganisms) for this potential power and, even, a caution with regard to any untrained attempt to manipulate actual change.

Philip Carr-Gomm puts what I've been trying to say above quite beautifully:

"even though Druidry is fundamentally a magical spirituality, books on Druidry usually avoid the subject of magic, and spellcraft is hardly ever mentioned. This is because the topic of magic can so easily generate 'glamour', and far from leading us closer to wisdom, can ensnare us in delusion.

The problem with the kind of magic that involves the casting of spells, aside from the danger of the misuse of power from insufficient psychological and ethical development, is that it is so easy for an interest in this activity to feed an attitude of consumerism that tempts people to fall yet again into the trap of believing that happiness or fulfilment will come from getting things or having things. The type of magical experience that Druidry fosters is quite the reverse – it is the type of experience you get when you trek out into the wilds of nature and you are overwhelmed with a feeling of awe that has nothing to do with owning or getting anything. When you can look at life, and experience that none of it belongs to you, quite magically and paradoxically you can feel then – in the depths of your being – that you truly belong in the world.[49]

I would like to close this chapter with one more 'dialogue' of my two inner voices, for the discovery that I have a wise old wizard inside me is just about the most magical thing to have happened to me. And he *never* attempts to change actual situations. His advice is always to show me another way of viewing it. I have to say that it was yet another time of immense darkness. Same old stuff – the shit that had landed on my lap after my decision was getting too much to bear. It was Remembrance Day but my head was so full off mess that I'd almost forgotten. It is expressed as a prayer to God... and a response!

Journal Notes - November 11th 2008 (Remembrance Day)

*Please God – what have I done? Why is it like this? Why do I have to live inside of such misery? I'm breaking up here... I need help... I need help... what do I do?*
   **Open the window.**
   *It's opened now and I can hear . . . so many sounds. Countless birds... some more discernable than others. The crow... and at least a dozen smaller birds' intermingled song. There's also the sounds of*

the road... not too far away. A truck a car or two. And the sky echoes another sound just then – a plane up there. High up carrying pilgrims and passengers to their destination. The dog's barks too.

**What can you feel?**

I can feel the breeze... the crisp cold wind on my face.

**And LOOK Mark – what do you see?**

I see the world outside... outside my own little world (in my head). I see everything being the way it ought to be... I see nature's magic taking care of itself without worry or stress or emotional pain. I see the far distance... the blue / grey sky and the sunlight reflected high up on the cloud edges. I see the trees – various kinds – evergreens reminding us of life even in the cold dark winter, and the orange brown leaves of the late autumn fall – the image of nature's constantly birthing, living and dying, birthing, living and dying. I see the homes of others who live in this area, each one a dwelling for humankind... tribal huts for families... some have herb and vegetable gardens... others have lovely neat flower beds... still others are just left to live their own way. I see the birds dancing... the crows that fly back and forth in front of me... stunning acrobats, with such grace and elegance. I see the smaller birds hunting for food and twigs.

I see so much life. Life that just goes on from one day to the next, being as it ought to be... living the way that nature intended.

**So Mark, little brother, little hurt and broken boy, where are you in all of this life?**

I guess I'm usually NOT part of it. I'm stuck in the wallow of my own head – wishing, regretting, planning, hoping, self-hating... escaping too. I find so many ways to escape life. And yet it's this being plugged in to life that I need so much.

**Mark remember all the lessons of the past... you don't need to try – or force this to happen. You just need to be... for the next few days allow yourself to let it all wash over you. Allow yourself to sense what's going on around you and feel part of it. You cannot control**

anything – you cannot force or manipulate or even demand by petitioning gods etc. All is as it is. The irony is that more begins to be yours when you rest and learn to see what is already there.

Nature has a mind Mark... align yourself to that mind – what you are doing MOST of the time is arguing with that mind... it's not as you want so you argue and say 'I want it like this or that'. Give up and let go of those big desires... learn, rather, to accept and love the smaller pleasures.

What do you really enjoy about life Mark?

I love bringing joy to others – bringing magic – enabling people to make sense of life, find meaning, construct ritual to help them come to terms with things, evoke their own inner magic and beauty.

You enjoy doing all that Mark because you also long for all those gifts that you give to others.

So how do I learn to give those gifts to myself?

You are right now, Mark, by giving time to your inner voice, your inner wisdom, you KNOW this already, and you have all the answers you need.

What else do you enjoy? What really excites you Mark?

Knowledge, learning, discovery, mystery, finding beauty, and then passing it all on.

Well maybe some of that magic should not be handed on so fast? Maybe you should let the magic work a little longer inside you before trying to pass it on?

That's something I used to say to myself when I worked as a priest. We are so busy (as preachers) learning new concepts and then handing them on that we fail to let them do their work in ourselves.

Good. You remember that. The same is true for what your vocation is now. Let the magic feed you. Let the studies feed you. Let the gwersu feed you. Live it... live inside it. Immerse yourself in it. Don't try to make it transform you. See it less as a body building enhancer and more as a natural fertilizer. Live like this more and more Mark and you will see miracles in other areas of your life –

even those parts that seem totally hopeless and out of control. Give yourself time. If your give yourself time... you will, ironically, have more time (and more wisdom) to naturally pass on anyway.

*Ok I do understand. I do.*

Now, this is hardest thing for you to grasp right now, your BIG problems, the one that drove you to this place today, the one that threatens to break you down yet again, is of your own making. You are trying to make life suit you, rather than learning to let you suit your life. You are constantly resisting what is. You are wishing and dreaming of the way you want it to be and thus failing to live with it as it is. NOTHING outside of your own experience is your business Mark. Nothing. You can't control other people's emotion, thoughts, and personalities. All you can do is live with how it is and learn to love the HOW of how it is. Do not fear the pain. Do not fear the 'thought' of the 'what if'. Look at what treasure you uncover when pain is actually allowed to run free, break the barriers and flow! Today you allowed that to happen and it has led you to your inner self. There was a lesson you once stumbled across that you expressed as 'learning to stay with the treasure'. That's where you should be Mark, and then this breaking point will not be required so much, for the treasure will not need digging up if you are already living within it. Live in the NOW with the WHAT IS and see the treasure that's there.

*But I find it so hard to see when I so often feel so cheated by life. I can't see gold but only mud.*

What is the difference is gold and mud Mark? Gold is something over which people fight and make war. Gold is something which, if you had in your hand, you would hold tightly so as not to lose it or let it be stolen from you. MUD is what we're made of. Mud is the dirty yet rich fertilizer of life. Mud is worth more than gold.

*But the mud and muck I refer to is my shattered dream... my place of desolation... the mess and muddle than I am sinking into.*

Then sink Mark. Sink but don't resist, let it take you where it wants to take you. If you let the things that you find so unpleasant *be your teacher, the mud will turn to gold. The secret is to live with those things that really cannot be changed. Size them up, see them for what they are... and then gracefully accept them... they will begin to lose their fearful power over you if you stop fighting them.*

*My gosh I've been so self-absorbed that I've only just remembered that it's Remembrance Day today.*

**Well don't start the self-punishing guilt trip Mark. This is another great lesson for you. Learn to look deeply – clearly at everything that happens – in the here and NOW – see it for what it is – and then ask yourself what lesson does it have for you? Just as the open window and the sights, sounds, and feeling helped plug you back in to this amazing living universe, ask yourself what 'suddenly remembering that it's Remembrance Day' can mean. This is what divination is Mark, looking for synchronicities and making sense of them. True 'seers' are those who can interpret apparent random co-incidences to what is going on in the NOW moment. Such seers do not use their divinatory skills as a narcotic to dull your senses and force you into more futuristic dreams, they wake you up to what's going on for you right now... with the possibility of real change right now... which (of course) effects the future. When you look at nature... and read it like a book, you are being a seer... the same is true for anything that you read and interpret... do not fear this ability... use it...**

*So what does the remembrance that it is Remembrance Day mean for me now?*

**It has come into your mind at this point, Mark, because to truly remember is to truly re-connect to everything that is. Not to go back in time and wallow, but to re-connect yourself to all your experiences. To allow them to be. Not to try and escape from them by futile dreaming, but live with the reality of them... and use their lessons for your current growth. To RE-MEMBER = to plug yourself back into your self. Your Member is your body. To re-connect you to you.**

*Oh my God!*

**Your God Mark is the voice of your deepest self. He/She/It is that**

*inner essence – that immanent wisdom, as well as the transcendent 'is-ness' of all things – the whole universe is God... and that includes you. If everything is as connected as you are discovering then why is it such a surprise to 'make connections' between all things? Believe it, live it, see, feel it, be it.*

I always used to say that I was a priest only in so much as everyone is a priest and I am a magician only in so much as everyone is a magician. My priesthood is there to enable others to discover their own priest-ness, and my magician-ship is there to enable others to discover their own inner magic. I'm still an ordained C of E priest, even if I now walk with Druids. But what does my priesthood mean to me now? And how do I express it?

# Chapter 12

# Post-denominational Priesthood!

*Being able to travel from this world to the next, the raven symbolizes also the power of healing – but the type of healing that comes through a radical confrontation with the unconscious, with the hidden, with the Shadow, and with the darker, potentially destructive aspects of the psyche. The raven's association with death becomes an association with depth and thus with depth psychology and the transformative powers of initiation – for such a moment marks to a greater or lesser extent the death of the old self, and the rebirth of a new self.*
Philip & Stephanie Carr-Gomm[50]

*I believe contemplation shows us that nothing inside us is as bad as our hatred and denial of it. Hating and denying it only complicates our problems. All of it is grist for the mill. Everything belongs. God uses everything. There are no dead ends. There is no wasted energy. Everything is recycled.*
Fr. Richard Rohr[51]

My priestly role in the community, which I thought was going to fade away to nothing, is being re-born, re-formed, re-created in a most remarkable way. Nature's recycling process is a profoundly beautiful symbol of human life. It says 'nothing is wasted,' 'everything is used,' even the shit. I want to describe, now, a particularly beautiful piece of re-cycled shit.

When I resigned as a Vicar I knew I would badly miss performing the services and rituals for the community – the baptisms, weddings and funerals, as well as the annual community celebrations like Christmas, Harvest and

Remembrance. It was very painful coming to terms with the fact that I would no longer be able to offer myself in this way. Then it happened, the inevitable. Six months after my decision to unbutton my dog-collar a woman whose son had taken his own life, and whose funeral I had been asked to officiate some years before, got in touch with me via the local funeral directors. Her husband had now died and she said she could only imagine me taking the ceremony. He was not a believer and she remembered that, when I took her son's funeral, I had respected the family's wishes not to talk religion. The widow asked the funeral directors to contact me, and they told me she was absolutely depending on me.

Well my initial reaction (apart from feeling moved that she'd asked me) was that the whole thing would be quite out of the question. I was no longer serving as a licensed priest; therefore she'd have to go the usual route of asking a local cleric to perform the ceremony. The only other possibility would be for her to contact a humanist and have a totally secular funeral.

Then memories of the woman's son and his service started to flood my mind. This family had been through so much. I'd been to see the husband a few weeks before he died – just as a friend – but I had no idea he would be gone in weeks. The inner arguments in my head were intense: 'No way Mark, you've left licensed ministry, and even if you were still able to officiate you're no longer a Vicar. You'd be treading on toes if you did this.'

'But Mark, this woman needs you. This family needs you. Bugger convention. Stick your cassock on one more time and do it for them.'

The inner debate started getting out of hand, so I sat down and tried to quieten the thoughts and allow myself to calm down. Gradually I was able to see that there was another way. I knew I couldn't pretend things were the same. I'd moved on, and I could not be a Vicar to a community where I no longer served as a

Vicar. But I could still be a spiritual friend for those who find themselves uncomfortable with formal religion and yet were not humanist!

I found the thought quite scary but also exiting. Could I? Could I do that? Could I quietly offer myself as something of a middle way between two worlds? I called the funeral director and he agreed that there was nothing stopping me from taking this service on those terms. So I agreed, and a whole new world opened up.

At the next available opportunity I sat down at my computer, opened Google, and searched for any other celebrants who were somewhere between these two worlds. I found plenty. I even found an umbrella organization that gave some support to such celebrants and joined it. It's called the Association of Independent Celebrants.

On top of these 'Soulful Ceremonies' (as I call them) I also offer myself for retreats and quiet days. I've led many over the last year, some of which were more specifically Christian and others of which were more eclectic. In many ways I still feel like a priest, but not a priest of Churchianity. This is something I recently wrote in my journal:

'I noticed something important today. A remarkable thing is happening. Having been ordained by an Anglican bishop into the church of God, I am still a priest, and that remains true forever. But I am finding myself drifting further and further from the notion of being a 'Churchian' priest and more an 'eclectic' or even simply 'human' priest – a priest of whoever needs me to articulate their spiritual needs in a ritual form… even if atheist. It seems like every culture has priesthoods. They spring up throughout history. Certain cultures created official priestly orders whereas others simply evolved out of the community's needs.

All communities have their ritual leaders – men and women who are somehow selected and then set apart to do the liturgical and *ritual things. I have found, over my ten years as a priest, that the vast majority of people who use the services of the established church, do not do so because they are believers in the Christian story, but simply need the ritual leader of the community to speak for them (symbolically) at this time of great need – birth, marriage, death etc. There is an innate pagan folk religion in people which often finds itself being expressed through these (sometimes) ill fitting Churchian ceremonies. I know some clergy who hate doing them. They feel some sort of resentment towards the families and often set up great hurdles as if they should not be asking for the Church's help. Of course, most priests are open-armed and welcome folk for the rites.*

*Myself? Well I used to say (and still believe) that these rites of passage or occasional offices, as they are called, are THE single most important thing a parish clergy person does in her or his ministry. On top of that we should never use them as opportunities to force our religious belief. These are tremendously important times for families… they need holding and caring for and enabling to express their deepest feelings (which may be gratitude to God) but not evangelizing. I used to unashamedly tailor-make my ceremonies for every individual in a way that suited them pastorally, theologically and emotionally. I cannot claim always to have got it right but I always did my best.*

When I was still a Vicar I used to adore shocking people who came to me expecting a 'no' by giving them an unconditional 'yes, yes, yes'. For example, couples who wanted to be married but had both been divorced, and in some cases, twice before. I saw their nerves mixed with child-like love, and would delight in saying 'of course I'll marry you'. Or the baptism couple who would love to invite their Buddhist friend as a god-parent but have heard that all godparents need to be confirmed, and if not then they must have certainly been baptised. 'Of course' I'd say. Or the woman whose son died of heroin and wanted me to read his 'poem to an addiction' which was full of hardcore swearing but made perfect sense. 'Of course,' I'd say. I always saw what we did as parish clergy to be the utmost privilege. How could we ever refuse someone a gift or a sacrament? The sacraments are often used to exclude rather than include. Is that really right? As I've said previously, I always saw the sacraments as signs of what already is rather than rituals that effect a change.

I once conducted an informal funeral ceremony for an old man's cat in the lady chapel of the great Priory church I served as Vicar. It was another strange mix of pagan-folk religion and establishment Christianity, and the two came together in a terrible clash that afternoon. I don't know how I did not totally lose it. The old man, who suffered from severe Parkinson's disease, was sat next to me facing the altar on which I'd lit a candle as a sign of his cat. He was crying as I said some prayers. Then there was a huge bang at the church porch and another elderly man walked in, crashing the door behind him. I knew at once who is was – the guy who's turn it was to lock up. He obviously noticed us up at the chapel because he shouted at top volume that he needed to lock up. I quickly tiptoed down to meet him and quietly explained what was going on, and suggested that he simply leave me lock up when I'd finished. *He stormed off.*

A week or so later the same man verbally attacked me in a meeting demanding an apology. Once more I explained that a poor bereaved man had come to me and needed someone to create a spontaneous little ritual for his cat etc. He just muttered 'you're bloody useless.' I can't pretend I wasn't angry, especially on behalf of the poor old man with the cat. I was fuming, but I turned away, and faced the committee secretary who absorbed my anger until I could continue with the meeting.

I do sometimes find it incredible how religion can create people who totally and utterly miss the point, time and time again. Yet I feel I failed that grumpy old bugger. I just wish I was able (during my time there) to gently enable him to see more of the unconditional love of the saviour figure whose image beamed down from all the stained glass in the church he served so faithfully.

Now, however, I do not have an institution telling me how to behave or how to do this or that ritual or blessing. I still miss it, immensely, but I am freer, happier, more myself *and more a priest than I ever was.*

# Chapter 13

# The Great Mosaic

*In the stories in the Gospels of the baptism of Jesus the Spirit of God is compared to a dove… I have compared it to a raven. I do not mean to be perverse. It is just that ravens, or one particular pair of ravens, have come to mean a great deal to me. Since 1996 a pair has nested, quite remarkably, right in the centre of Chester, and for most of those years on the tower of the Cathedral, with the nest in full view of my study window. I have celebrated the Eucharist of an early morning surrounded by a large silence broken only by the faint honking of ravens. I have seen the adults displaying, or weaving the basket of their nest. I have looked through my telescope, set up in my study window, at the full-grown young flexing their wings. One year I caught the moment when one of the young took its first flight. They are extraordinary birds, and still my hearts leaps every time I see them, or hear them call. They show me something of God.*
Trevor Dennis[52]

So, what's left of my understanding of God, Christ, Divinity etc.? For years I'd been drifting from a purely Christian point of view. Now, having found a new expression of spirituality - a more open, nature based and magical one - how has my belief in God altered?

In order to answer that I will need to momentarily step back into the Christian framework, for how I have always understood the various denominations within the Church offers a clue to how I now see things within a wider ecumenism. I began this book by reminiscing about my first sermon as a newly ordained curate. My first sermon as a Team Vicar is similarly significant. Holding up a crystal prism I preached on the vastness and uncontain-ability of God. To the shock of some of the worshippers I let the crystal hang there for a while, twisting and turning on the end of its chain as I provocatively said, 'this crystal has a message for you'. I went on to describe how, when a single beam of pure white light is shone through the crystal, it refracts and pours out the other side in seven vibrant colours - the seven colours of the light spectrum that we see inside a rainbow, a soap bubble or a pool of oil spilt on the floor. I used it as a symbol of how the pure white light of The Divine is simply too rich, too vast, too much for any single tradition to fully contain. All each tradition can do is add its own colour to the picture, so each of the colours, together, creates the *big* picture. I went on to ascribe the various colours to the various denominations of the Church, stating that dodgy ecumenism tries to make us all conform - water down to the lowest common denominator, where we end up with a dull greyness. However, a mature ecumenism lets the reds be red, and the greens be green. It does not attempt the futile dream of complete uniformity. We need to see the beauty of each colour, *for the colour is the colour of God*. And we will see a bigger picture of the divine if we don't try to harmonise and make it all work together etc.

I preached that we ought to learn how to truly value each and every tradition, even the ones we find so difficult. It was an essential message for that particular church, for it had all the various traditions within it. I said that the fragmentary nature of Christianity, though in some ways a curse, is also a gift because each of the fractures occurred when the vision got too big for the particular group to hold on to. So a new group splintered off – making new colours.

I preached that we cannot and should not simply combine it all and make one great Christian faith. We need to see each broken group as owning a gift – an insight into God. I love the mess. I feel we deny ourselves so much when we have to tidy it all up. Every human person is blessed and loved by God and each responds to Him / Her / It in a different way. We don't need to label and box religious experience. *Every church denomination contains part of the colour and glory that, when seen together, makes up the whole light spectrum of God. I thank God for the denominations and the differences, the contradictions and the messiness. I thank God for it all, because it's where He lives. This is what I preached.*

Essentially I still hold the same view but with reference to global spiritually rather than just Christian spirituality. I feel that each faith or spiritual path offers a nugget of truth – a pearl of wisdom. I imagine an enormous circular mosaic, made up of literally millions of coloured stones, and I see more being added as folk from different cultures and backgrounds walk up to the circumference, kneel down and reverently add their own stone, their own insight, their own gift. It is, of course, a messy and muddled mosaic, erratic and not all in harmony or unified. Some of the stones clash badly, some of them are jagged and harsh, some of them make sense to certain groups but do not to others.

This is what I see as being a great mosaic or web of deity. It also means that I can hold on to the great gift of the many insights my own Christian story has given me over the years, for though the Church drives me mad at times, its founder still has a sweet and powerful place in my heart.

Journal Tues 12<sup>th</sup> Aug 2008. DEEP INSIGHT

*As I sit here I'm aware of nature's subtle sounds: birds chattering, wind blowing through trees, each part of it celebrating its place in the Great Mosaic. Spirits are everywhere, as part of this huge orchestra of deity. Have I become a pantheist? Do I now see the divine in everything?*

*Something else has occurred to me too. I've prayed all my life. My prayers took on a new meaning in 1986 when I became a Pentecostal. Since then it has developed and changed as I have grown and expanded theologically and spiritually. During some* periods it has been deeply personal and very human, and at other times (particularly my more eastern mystical times) it's been more ethereal. During my AA years my prayers were to the Higher Power. They are changing again into a more pagan / nature based way. What occurred to me is that as I change, and as my prayer changes, God also changes, or my experience of him / her does. It's not that I replace one god with another but that I develop a new insight into the One God. This is perhaps where I differ from the majority of Pagan Druids. Most of them think in terms of a whole pantheon of individual gods and goddesses. I guess I see them all as manifestations of the One – the Uncreated One – the Great Spirit. I also see this Great Spirit as existing in fragmentary forms within and throughout all of nature.

So Great Spirit – where am I going? Who am I? Who are you?

**Mark, son-brother, come back to me. Pause, feel, experience, don't rush or run or try to work it all out – you return to me (and your deepest Self) by stopping. You have been on another necessary climb of the ladder... the time has come once more to fall back down into me... yet it is a renewed vision of me you now return to. That is where you go now. I am waiting as I always am – waiting, watching, loving, holding. I am the motherly / fatherly One who waits for the son / daughter's return. Never lose sight of these precious insights – they are gifts. Do not think that your Christian past must all now be forgotten. You can no longer remain within the institution but the gifts you have been given can and should be held on to for where you are now to live – do not be confused. You still have this voice – it is here within you whenever you travel. You, Mark, are a part of God. You, Mark, are your own answer. You, Mark, and I are One. We are One and we are many – we are the essence of deity within all things. Do not fear. You DO know me Mark, trust your deepest voice – trust your innermost insights. It does not all have to fit neatly in place. Learn from where you find wisdom but do not force yourself to fit inside any box of interpretation. Openness is a gift you always held on to as a Christian**

*priest. Keep this open spirit as you now travel a christo-druidic path. Use what works for you, disregard what doesn't. Love your past, present and future for it is all part of the journey and it is all good. Everything belongs.*

Of course all god language is metaphor. A very useful exercise for thinking about notions of gods and deity is to ask yourself what myths and metaphors you use? What makes sense for you? What's your mythology? The great mythologist, Joseph Campbell, describes finding our mythology as a pathway to bliss. Myths locate us. I see my own dis-location of the last half-decade (or more) as being a gradual dissatisfaction with the traditional Christian mythology. Part of the problem with the Christian myth is that we're taught to literalize so much of it.

One of the great moments of enlightenment, for me, came when I saw a pattern in my own religious journey – something I can detect as I look back over my life. Whenever I literalize a myth I end up disenchanted. The great gust of excitement I experience as I 'find' a new way (i.e. Pentecostalism) gives way to a feeling of being let down, when the now literalized 'new path' shows itself to be less than perfect. Now, there are folk in each of the paths I've encountered who can happily exist inside that culture / mythology in a pretty literal way (Pentecostals, Anglo-Catholics, even liberal intellectuals) and can see their way as true *factually*. For them the myths have become facts. Yet that's all they have - a factualised myth.

This is where I get stuck. I want more, so I go through some period of confusion, disenchantment and breaking apart. Until I realize (for the umpteenth time) that what I have found is not a factual truth but a mythic truth. Joseph Campbell points out that there is the personal and the transcendent. I now look at myths as pointing beyond themselves to the transcendent. Druidry is a mythic path for me – as is Christianity. And I can hold them both together so long as I don't literalize them – their myths meet on the other side. The cosmic Christ – the gods of place etc. My new Quest is to find a mythology for *now*.

I notice there is tenseness and relaxedness when it comes to faith / beliefs. I recognize it inside myself: one comes from ego the other from Self. When I literalize the faith experience, it naturally becomes tense because I want to cling to it and possess it – it is small, threatened and personal. But when I see the belief as universal and beyond the literal I relax – I do not need to control, defend, grasp. I think of Emma Restall-Orr who simply smiles when folk want her to get defensive about her beliefs and argue a case for them. Faith (god) is indefensible because is it experienced in the mythic part of our awareness. All we have is symbolic language – yet to say 'all we have' is not to downplay it. We have a power-filled symbolic language which connects us to the mystery beyond, within and around all things… the great mystery – the great mosaic.

Journal notes:

*All Saints Church, 17th Feb 2008. It was lovely to go to Church today, with all the sounds, smells and statues of high church worship, but it occurred to me that I could have been in almost any religious ritual of any religion. The power of the experience was in the setting and symbols rather than the doctrines and ritual language. I've been inside Hindu Mandirs, Buddhist Temples, Sikh Gudwaras, Jain Temples, Moslem Mosques, Catholic Shrines, Pagan Stone Circles, and Native American prayer huts. I could have been in any one of them today. They all point to the same reality - from beyond themselves to the Great Mosaic.*

In the next chapter I shall continue with this theme of the god/dess who alludes all literal description and relies on human metaphors and mythology to be spoken about but, rather than looking for glimpses out there (a transcendent god), we will turn our gaze inwards and find our magic (divinity) within. And, as I have said so many times before, it is within and through our inner woundedness and brokenness – rather than our success and perfections - that we truly find this light of deity.

# Chapter 14

# The god/dess in YOU!

*I open myself to breathe the air, the skies, once again, conscious of the vague figures of ancestors watching, conscious of an old raven perched on the stone behind me. Or is that me... For a brief moment I have two sets of eyes.*
Emma Restall Orr[53]

*One of the most moving moments that can occur on our spiritual and psychological journey is the discovery that in our hearts lies a wounded child. However careful our upbringing might have been, it seems inevitable that we first experience this inner child as hurt and rejected. Once, however, we open ourselves to him or her, no longer pretending or living as if s/he didn't exist, we find that a further level peels away, to reveal that the child within is in fact a Divine child, a radiant seed-being of God/dess. Within a Christian framework we can say that we experience the reality and the presence of the Christ-child within our hearts. The Druid tradition speaks of the same mystery, but calls the child the Mabon.*
Philip Carr-Gomm[54]

It was my daughter's birthday recently and we decided to take her and my son to see Mary Poppins at the theatre. It was a magical and enchanting show, and also a revelation. I'm afraid I'm used to carrying a notebook and pencil with me almost everywhere now because I so often collect inspirational quotes and anecdotes from everyday encounters. Of course it can be tiring for members of my family to see me scribbling when I should be enjoying a show with them, but it just happens.

There is a scene in Mary Poppins that, no matter how many

times I have watched the film version, never jumped out at me like it did on this occasion. The father of the children who Mary Poppins nannies, is a spoilt brat and a killjoy. He has allowed himself to completely deny and repress his own inner child. He is now in the all too serious world of adult business and banking etc. He cannot – will not – allow anything to break through the wall of perfectionism and respectability that he's built around himself. He shows no emotion to his wife or children and does not know how to relate to them. He cannot play and even views his children's games as pointless and something from which to grow up. It is a very sad picture, made even sadder when we learn that, partly responsible for this man-made monster, was his own traumatic childhood. He had been badly bullied by his nanny and grew up fearing adults, fearing the world and needed to protect himself against any further breaking or bullying. Ironically he'd turned into something of a bully himself.

The scene I refer to is quite remarkable. There is a precious vase above the door in the hall, a family heirloom worth enough to bail them out should things ever get financially unviable. There it stands – high and exalted – a mirror image of the proud and pompous man himself, outwardly perfect and quite impregnable. The vase, in the father's opinion, is there to rescue him should he need to reach out for its help. And he's quite right about that, for the vase is indeed potentially able to rescue him, but not from financial ruin, rather from the prison he has put himself within. It is the symbolic key to unlocking his own happiness – the re-discovery of his own broken yet beautiful inner child.

This is what happens. Something goes wrong that causes the unthinkable. Something dislodges the vase and it wobbles and then falls to the floor, smashing on impact. It is a tragic moment. You expect him to explode with rage and despair. Then the most amazing thing occurs. He stoops down, speechless at the spectacle of his priceless vase in fragments and falls on his knees to gather up the pieces. But he sees something. There, among the broken porcelain, are the tiny shining stars that he had hidden there years and years before, while still an enchanted little boy who loved to look into the night sky at the celestial twinkling lights. He quietly started gathering them up and, with every one retrieved, regained a little bit more of that inner child he'd tried to repress for so long. The beauty – the sheer metaphorical genius – of this scene is that it took a fall, a breakage, of something materially priceless, to recover something psychologically priceless. The wounded and bullied little boy, now rediscovered, was the key to this man's own mental survival. He was now well on the way to full re-enchantment. Soon he would, for the very first time, be out in the park flying kites with his own children.

This rings enormous bells with my own journey. Over time I have begun to understand myself in a new way. The sense of me always needing approval – always feeling underneath everything and everyone – always frightened of the 'grown ups' etc. comes from the little boy who's trapped inside me. Unlike the father in Mary Poppins my own shell and self-protection has never been as strong so the little hurt boy comes to the surface often. He feels everything's too much. He can't cope and wants to be rescued. He waits to be abandoned and rejected again and again!

All this I have known for years but recently I had new revelation. There is also a 'grown up' – projected adult voice inside us too. A larger, but essentially equally egotistic immature adult voice – the mirrored company of voices of my past who've been critical and harsh / rather than critically constructive. So there's a little boy inside me who never grew up. And there's a grown up inside me who does not know how to deal with the little boy. He continues to scold and shout at the little chap (just like the grown up voices in the past).

My revelation was that just as I am able to hold, love, tolerate, forgive and heal other 'little children' (adults who've come to me to talk about problems etc.), so I can learn to be that calm, caring, counsellor towards my own wounded inner self.

Journal notes:

> *I heard a new 'Voice' today. The trauma of the last few hours has been intense. Sometimes I don't know what to do with the pain I inflict on myself. But today – after the most severe turmoil and fear – I heard another 'me'. I was in bits and feeling just about as hopeless as a man could. I heard myself saying 'ok – wizard where are you? Where's your wisdom?' and another part of me remembered my spiritual father, Richard Rohr's advice, 'Don't run from it - stay with the pain – and let it transform you.' So I just wept and wept until I heard my deep inner self say this:* **'Mark, you feel everyone's against you… everyone's out to get you… life's a great big monster movie and you need to win the approval of every character in it. But Mark it's not their approval you need. No Mark you don't need to look for the approval, forgiveness, love or compassion of others – you need to love yourself! You need to forgive yourself. You need to heal yourself by being a big brother to yourself who lets his little brother sob in his arms and receive the love and acceptance he's always longed for.**

The Druid tradition has helped me to see that this little boy inside me, not only needs to be listened to and loved without judgment, but is a *divine child* – a spark of god, a glimpse of pure gold. Druid chief, Phillip Carr-Gomm, has a powerful and moving ability to weave together insights from the Druid, Christian and Psychological traditions. What he says of this wounded divine child is profound:

'In a peculiar reflection of the story of the Prodigal Son, it is we as adults who turn to the Child to recognise him as the manifestation of Divinity within us. And it is we as adults who come to understand that the negativity and the destruction that we experienced and expressed came from the desperation of the wounded child who needed to be heard. In our struggle to 'grow up' we ignored the voice that became buried deeper and deeper in our hearts.'[55]

Of course, it is not just the wounded inner child in each of us who is divine. The awe-inspiring wonder is that each one of us is in fact a reflection of god/dess. As a Christian priest I always used to love enabling folk to discover what I called their inner-God-ness. This is nothing whatsoever to do with inner-*good*-ness. It is the spark of deity – the divine mark that those from biblical traditions call 'being made in the image and likeness of God'. I see (and still see) the Christ role as that of bringing people back to their divine selves... their very essence.

A person's essence is the indestructible self and, once we learn to live from that place, we're capable of real magical living. Not in the sense of making things appear out of nowhere, but living in such a way as to see the magic – the divine - in everything and every situation. It is the pure gold of our truest selves.

Spiritual people can point you to it, holy religions can help map the way, psychology can strip away the layers that cover it, and myths can give a language to express it, but only you can truly find it – for it is you. It is your truest self and it is glorious.

Simon Parke expresses this so beautifully:

*'To this extent no one can teach you anything about being human. Your essence itself knows already all there is to know. It understands and already is, more than anyone can speak of. Already, in your potential, you surpass the wise sayings of any guru, enlightened one, or prophet. These people can startle, provoke or point you towards your essence, but they must then back away, and shade their eyes – for your essence outshines them.'*[56]

# Chapter 15

# A Re-Enchanted reading of Christianity

*A bird, or so it seemed, was tumbling in the wind, playing with its soaring, swirling currents. She had all the freedom of the air and more. It was as if she gave the sky its freedom, and so indeed she did. For at the beginning, when the world was made, she had untied the sky from earth's weight, to let it float high and wide, a playground for the angels and herself, for divine somersaults and cartwheels. She flew above us now, the raven-black Spirit of God, turned on her back for a second, for the sheer fun of it, and gave us a soft call of recognition.*
Trevor Dennis[57]

*One basic datum underlies every religion under the sun, the principle of Incarnation. The Word or Logos, God's self-expression made manifest, has given the light of its divine spark to every mind/soul coming into the world. Christians call this the Christ or "Christ in us." Other faiths have different names or modes of expression for this same inner reality.*
Tom Harpur[58]

Journal notes:
*Easter 2008*
   *Well this was the first Holy Week and Easter that I have not attended church in about 23 years. I was 18 when I first stepped onto the Christian road and have never missed Easter since then. This year I decided to take my children to a celebration of the Spring Equinox instead. I'm not sure why, but I simply didn't need Easter this year. It's certainly not that I suddenly disbelieve everything about the Jesus story. Far from it. It's more that I do not equate his*

*story with the Church anymore. So who is Jesus to me?*

*The Christ is the 'word' – the logos (close to wisdom / Sophia) – the God who speaks. Jesus (who I feel I can know through this Christ spirit) was a human face of God. There are many faces of God. The power of Jesus' parables and his humble spirit still moves me deeply. The prodigal son still makes the hairs on the back of my neck stand up. But Jesus is not the sole property of the Church, just as The Buddha is not the property of the Tibetans, and the Greek Myths are not the property of the Greeks alone. All these myths and metaphors are for the benefit of all humankind.*

Since leaving the officialdom of the Church as an institution I've had plenty of time to think through some of the questions that have bothered me for some time. I've also been able to gather and devour piles of books from all sorts of faith, tradition and philosophy. Some of them fall into the category of what I call 'Cosmic Christianity' or even 'Pagan Christianity'. The latter might seem a contradiction of terms. However the books I refer to have helped me to recover a missing element of the Christ story, which is also a miraculous bridge to my new magical and nature based spirituality.

Here is not the place to go into these theories. However should anyone reading these words care to treat themselves to a potentially liberating read, do go and get a copy of The Jesus Mysteries by Tim Freke and Peter Gandy or The Pagan Christ by Tom Harpur. But be warned – they might change the way you look at everything!

Tom Harpur kindly gave me permission to quote his beautiful *Seven Principles of Cosmic Spirituality:*

The entire cosmos is the manifestation of Divine Mind-every molecule, every cell, every creature, every rock, tree, mountain, planet, blazing star, whirling galaxy and universe of galaxies.

We are all an integral, interconnected part of the whole cosmos and our own inner world is a holograph of the cosmos within us.

One basic datum underlies every religion under the sun, the principle of Incarnation. The Word or Logos, God's self-expression made manifest, has given the light of its divine spark to every mind/soul coming into the world. Christians call this the Christ or "Christ in us." Other faiths have different names or modes of expression for this same inner reality.

Every religion whose ethical core is summed up by the word "compassion" or "loving-kindness" to all other creatures without exception has a vision of the truth and is a valid "way" to Transcendence.

No one faith or religion-whatever its claims may be, alone has The Truth.

True cosmic spirituality is steeped in, flows from, and derives its most powerful analogies and metaphors from the natural world – from the tiniest bit of dust to the spiraling stars above.

The core aim of cosmic spirituality is radical transformation, both personal and societal.[59]

In the next section we will see how a wonderful collection of people, from all walks of life and from all over the world, deal with these two (seemingly opposing) worlds of nature-based spirituality and Christianity. While not all the contributors still see themselves as Christian, many of them manage to take the heavy and burdensome rock - that much of Churchianity has become - and delicately chisel out some beautiful insights into the person of Jesus. I hope you find their words as inspiring and encouraging as I have.

# Part 3

# 'Tales from Beyond the Magic Doorway'

*What if*
*Jesus and Merlin were to meet*
*At twilight*
*In the garden, in the grove,*
*One looking forward to the Skull of Golgatha,*
*One looking back on the Sacred Head of Bran?*

*What would they say to one another,*
*These men, these gods,*
*Who live in time beyond their lives —*
*One forward, one retrograde?*

*"Let this Cup pass from me..." says the one.*
*"May the earth open and swallow me,*
*May the sky fall upon me,*
*May the sea rise and cover me,*
*May fires consume me..." says the other.*

*"Take this cup and drink from it..." says the one.*
*"This is the Cauldron of Inspiration and Wisdom..." says the*
*other.*
*"Do this in remembrance..." says the one.*
*"I know the Cup*
*From which the wave has overflowed.*
*I know the end of the dawn..." answers the other.*

*What if they do meet*
*There in the grove, in the garden,*
*Two avatars —*
*One about to ascend,*

*One about to descend —*
*Each serving the Chalice in his way?*

*What if Merlin's Affallanau and Jesus' Rood is the same Tree?*
*One rides it to his destiny,*
*One sits beneath to prophesy.*

*What could they give to one another*
*These prophets circling in their Time-long orbits?*
*Could Merlin say: "The seed is planted, the tree will grow*
*There is a thorn in Avalon that bears fruit in thy name."*
*Would Jesus reply wistfully: "Kiss Nimue for me.*
*Tell her I love her beauty and her power."*
RoMa Johnson, 2004

I decided to call this final section *Tales from Beyond The Magic Doorway*, because to read this collection of personal stories is to enter a magical world. Each has been kindly offered by a fellow traveller who was willing to share their story of personal enchantment. Some began their journey within the Christian tradition. A few are still within it. All have found, within nature-based spirituality, a rich source of wisdom and a fully enchanted vision of the universe.

The stories are divided into four groups: *Celtic Christians* are those that see themselves as fully Christian but deeply connected to the pre-Christian Celtic world. *Christo-Druids* are those who have a primarily Christian understanding of God, yet are also plugged in to a Druidic spirituality. The *Pagan-Druids* are those who see themselves as fully pagan yet also have a deep respect for the person of Jesus. And there is a final section which I have called *The American Indians and the Celts*. I have long detected an immense connection between pre-Christian Celtic culture and that of the tribes of the (Native) Americas. With this in mind the final section includes three stories from that perspective.

I have tried to introduce each contributor as best I can however, because Celtic Christianity and Paganism is (in places) still so misunderstood, some of them (understandably) did not want their full identities to be given. Also you will see that some of them (especially the Pagan-Druids) have taken a 'Druid Name'. These are in brackets after their official name.

I offer these not out of any attempt to convince or convert. Indeed, not all the views and opinions you are about to encounter are ones I would subscribe to myself. Further, I'm sure that it would be quite impossible to totally harmonise them. But that is not the purpose of this section. I am not interested in a quest for harmonisation or uniformity. I am, rather, simply delighted and encouraged when I see how various people, the world over, have been able to tap into and make sense of such rich systems of believe.

And to the authors of these remarkable pieces - thank you! They have been a joy and a privilege to read and will, I'm sure, bright light and life to many others.

Chapter 16

# Celtic-Christians

*When Christianity first came to the British Isles, it was recognised as having a distinctly Celtic flavour. It was characterised by a continued reverence for Nature as the face of the Divine. The One God spoke simply in the solitudes of wind and woodland, sea-wave and mountaintop... and for centuries, the old Gods and Goddesses – the many faces of The One – continued to have a place in the hearts and the hold days of the people.*

*The Living Celtic Spiritual Tradition contains the beat of the earlier mystery tradition of Druidism, an intimate, immanent relationship to the Divine and a deep faith in the transformative power of Love, all leading towards Christ-consciousness. It honours the Earth as Divine Manifestation, the Mother of mystical experience, the hollow of God's hand. Its priests are called Ceile De–*

*The Companions or Spouses, of God.*
The Ceile De[60]

The Revd. Tess Ward is an Anglican Priest who works as a Hospice Chaplain and spiritual director. Her book, The Celtic Wheel of the Year (O Books), is a glorious feast of daily prayers and fascinating insights from the Pagan and Christian Celtic worlds. This is her story.

## How the Earth blessed me with the love of God
I was ordained in 2000 and had been sent to a suburban rural parish for my curacy. For a city girl the new place was strange. I did not share the aspirations of the others who had descended on these villages, wanting to be rid of the city and to set up their family homes with like-minded people. The churches did not

want much change, apart from higher attendance of course. That is how it began and that is how it went on for 3 years. I would stand up at the front and say things that I used to edit in my head when I was sat in a pew at the back. Words matter to me and they were not the words I would use - I did not want them in my mouth.

Across the road from the church was a wood and some fields. Every day I would go there with my collie dog (a pup in spirit) who'd round up every deer, muntjac, pheasant, rabbit, squirrel and even snake. When I first used to go, I'd get terribly lost. Woods have no paths. It was quite frightening to have no idea how to get out even though you knew you'd got in. Dante's words used to play over and over.

*Midway in the journey of our life*
*I found myself in a dark wood,*
*for the straight way was lost.*

I was in my late 30s and the straight way was becoming more and more lost. It did not seem the right way any more though I should say that my straight way had always been somewhat crooked. My inner mystical journey as a woman had always been in tension with the man-made church. When I was ordained I believed my call was to hold that tension, because I knew it was a tension for others too – both men and women. The one-size was no longer fitting all (if it ever had). In the wood there were no words, no language excluding me with every breath, no structures that did not fit the shape of my walk with God, just the breeze and the song of the birds. The only structures were the tall vault of trees, soft barked pines, oaks, beech, all manner of trees through different parts of the wood and a stream running through, where Georgie (my dog) would drink. And I could drink in that place. There, my longing was held and heard and there was the possibility of healing. As the months went on, I began to find my way. The trees did not accompany me. They offered no wise words. They just solidly were. They were just there when I needed to not be asked questions, not to come up with some terrific sermon, not even to intercede, just to be. And Georgie led me. So often I could not define what was happening inside but she would jump up, put her paws round me and look at me with her warm brown eyes, demanding no more than I love and be loved.

Throughout all of this, though I have doubted God's presence before in my life, I knew God was there. The more the old house of my faith was being dismantled, the more the wood became the home of my soul. As a Buddhist saying has it "barn's burnt down, now I can see the moon". God was showing me the simplicity of love when across the road in the church, I felt a long way from home. The trees and my dog taught me that nothing is separate. It hurt me that the church and the wood felt separate but more than that, I knew I was being led in the wood into a deeper place and that I had to go. The life of the church may return to me but it was not for now and I knew instinctively that while I was in role leading a church, I was neither free to explore life without it or assess what part it would play in my future.

I saw more than I had ever seen before what Christ meant. I was aware of my brokenness and so I knew what it was like to know my need of mercy. Deeper and wider and longer than that, though, was the reality of God's love which felt much more universal than it had sometimes been portrayed to me. This became the limit of my theology and even now, some years later, in happier times, my theology has still not recovered any sophistication. We are all connected. We are One with each other, with the earth and with the Spirit of God. We are loved. Our task is to love but things get in the way and we do not always manage that well. We are connected in this too. So we stand as one in need of mercy and in being held in the deep love that holds all. Christ came to show this, though many people who do not know Christ do know the love of God.

After my curacy, I came back home to Oxford. Along with not being the vicar anymore, the tension between the integrity of my spiritual life and institutional Christianity, finally snapped. I knew returning to parish life would be toxic at this point and did not know whether that was temporary or permanent. Interestingly, though, I held it before God every day. I believed in my priesthood and, fortunately, so did others. Although I was not part of a congregation I worked as a chaplain in the arts and in health.

In the summer between my curacy and settling back in Oxford, I went on holiday. Without thinking, I raided my bookshelves for all the books I had wanted to read but hadn't had time to. They were all about earth spirituality. I read the words "she" and "her" over and over again and they were like drops of water to my parched soul. The constant message, that my body was good and to be celebrated, went deep. The love for rock and tree and bird and flower was naturally part of the same celebration. This was not entirely new because all my adult life I had pursued my spirituality through woman writers that were not Christian, because they were the only ones that described my journey. I had laid them alongside many of the Christian mystics and together they had made sense of my experience. This is still true for me.

However, over the next few years I became aware that there was what might be an unbridgeable gap between them. The women spirituality writers, as one voice of several strands, speak of a woman emerging over her journey and becoming stronger and stronger in herself. Paradoxically, the more that this happens and the less she is beholden to other people's needs, the more connected with other people and the earth she becomes. The more she knows that she and her body are one with other people, the earth and Spirit, the more she can grow into freedom and who she is truly meant to be. This can be symbolized in practice with the circle and the space (i.e. a circle of people and silence in the middle). So people find their own voice, rather than being led with one voice which may or may not speak for all. The mystics allude to the discovery of the same Oneness - the same silence. However, it is not talked about in terms of becoming stronger in self (though that is the end result) but by letting go into the love of God through Christ. The process is similar to trusting the silence at the centre of the circle.

This is still not entirely resolved for me. I believe both however, pragmatically, as soon as Christ comes into the picture, we are back in the land of "hes" and "hims" and a language about surrender and "not me but him" that is not always healthy for a spiritually growing woman. Theologically I believe that Christ is an icon for humanity and not gender but even then, this icon feels very different if God came as a sexually active woman bearing children. This remains work in progress and as I believe that truth is paradoxical, I can live with the opaqueness.

Meanwhile as I began to learn the names of things in the garden and field and to pay attention to the seasons and plunge my hands in the soil and feel nature's healing, I searched for a group with whom to celebrate the Celtic Wheel. After a year 5 women came together and now, 4 years later, we are an evolved group of 7. We do different things every time we meet but there are some regular features. We always open and close the circle and call the directions and elements: Spirits of South (fire), West (water), North (earth), East (air) and Spirit at centre and through all. We always meet outside and we always have a fire. We always share our journeys. In between we might chant, drum or devise a simple ritual in relation to the season. We often make something too, like a wreath or a Brigid's Eye[61] with natural things.

After only 4 years, the eight festivals[62] have become as embedded in my spiritual rhythm as the Christian ones which have been with me for much longer. The Christian festivals were deliberately overlaid on the festivals celebrating the journeys of the sun and moon so, for me, to keep both feels natural. For most of the year this harmony produces a real richness, but in some cases the Celtic festivals are more meaningful to me than the Christian ones. Samhain[63] is more what I have always wanted All Souls to be and the Winter Solstice[64] is a more appropriate climax to 4 weeks of an Advent journey than what Christmas has become in our culture and churches. I love it that Imbolc[65] redeems Candlemas and celebrates a feisty saint/goddess in Brigid rather than celebrating Mary's purification because child-birth was seen to be unclean.

I have now returned to a small contemplative sacramental and new congregation. Four years on church cannot be the same for me. I don't share many of the concerns. The return to gendered language is hard, especially in a church full of people younger than me. But most of all, I cannot enter the conversations deciding who is "in" and who is "out", either in this little church or the vicious playing out of the wider one. It goes against my religion. As Julian of Norwich said, "Love was the meaning". Just trying to live that is task enough.

## How the Earth has blessed me
Although I am only a beginner at learning the secrets the earth has to share she has already taught me much about God.

## Nature – God's Direct Connection
I think most people have many of their spiritual moments in nature because it takes them back to the truth that we are all one and that there is a sacred connection between God and all living things. Christianity is at a disadvantage because we do not induct people into it through prayer (ie direct experience of God through practice) but through the Bible/doctrine. So people have to take a step away from life, absorb a story from a 2,000 year-old culture, and then hope the Holy Spirit relates it to their life.

Imposing doctrine from on high upon nature can feel unnatural, but it can also result in judging bodies and nature and dividing them from other parts of creation, which I find contrary to the way of the love, healing and wholeness seen in Jesus. The directness of nature, which as announces our place in the extended family of creation, means there is no theology needed to judge the experience. The task is simply to allow ourselves to be present to that reality.

## Nature – Incarnation

The physicality of the Earth is immensely important to me. The Celts said that Nature was their text. Christianity is a religion of the book. As a rather "head" dominated person a book religion isn't necessarily good for my soul. I have gained so much from being part of sacred rituals that use my body as well as my soul and, apart from the odd poem, do not involve books. There is as much doing as speaking. Though none of them would call themselves Christian, it is this group of women who live out what incarnation means, without thinking or speaking about it.

## Nature - the Wildness of God

For me, both the open-air rituals and nature itself express the wildness of God. The Centuries of liturgy have domesticated God, and I say that as a lover of liturgy! It has also made God one step removed rather than directly amongst the things of Creation. I will never forget celebrating my first summer solstice and walking round the brow of a hill and seeing a huge pink moon hanging low in the sky. Silence was the only response.

There is something about this distrust of direct experience, of our bodies and sexuality that makes the Christian culture grey and dull. With the exception of Pentecostal and Eastern Orthodox churches, Christian gatherings can feel tired and tawdry. It is almost as if life is squeezed out of everything. Honouring the earth with colour, creativity and experience seems a much more vibrant way of celebrating the life of God.

## Nature – Under the Same Sky

The outside world is something that we all share, whatever our creed or colour. In most of the world's religions, festivals celebrate the seasons of nature. In my work I have found that when I talk about spirituality in relation to nature, I have a language which people understand and respond to. It is similar when I talk about it in relation to psychology or human under-standing. However, when I talk about Christ so much needs to be de-familiarized and then re-told because he has become synonymous with conservatism, intolerance and an outmoded privileged power. It was out of a desire to express the depth of Christian mysticism with the breadth of Earth spirituality and show they are not as divided as they are sometimes perceived, that I wrote my prayer book "The Celtic Wheel of the Year" (O-Books 2007)

## Nature – Death and Darkness

I am still a Christian because to be held by God in the love and mercy shown in Christ, is a grace I need to return to on a daily basis. Our brokenness as well as being made for love connects us. However, I have not missed the word "sin" occurring in every section of a sacred gathering or even the constant focus on death. Even though losing someone can be so painful death is part of life. This is how it is seen in the Wheel, which seems truer to my experience. Earth spirituality, nature itself and Christian mysticism are all positive about darkness: that new things grow in the dark, that the dark and the light are necessary, that God is deep within the darkness as well as the light, that death will bring new life. There are some expressions of Christianity that do not recognize this and seek to banish darkness but my experience tells me that the Earth and the mystics are to be trusted. It was in the middle of the dark wood that I learnt the depth of God's love. The Spirit blew through the trees and whispered to me.

Heike Killet lives in Belgium and works with her husband in a small church whilst earning a living as a call centre operator. They have three children. Heike describes herself as a Celtic Christian and has found many deep insights through learning of the Ceile De community (an ancient Celtic-Christian spiritual tradition)[66]

## Heike's story

As a child, I used to be restless inside. I knew there was a dimension missing in my life but I couldn't find it for a long time. So in the end, I gave up searching. When I was older, my search restarted and finally I found an answer when one evening I desperately cried out to the God I didn't know and didn't believe in. From that moment on, warmth was in my heart and I knew that my cry had been answered. As I had friends in Christian circles, I started going to a church and found a friendly and caring community and some more answers to my many questions. My life changed a lot over the next years and I decided that my priorities also had to change. I wanted to live fully for this God whom I was gradually getting to know.

Over the years I settled into a Christian lifestyle and started sharing my discoveries. At the same time, without knowing it, I adopted a Christian jargon and imagery that narrowed my experiences and understanding quite significantly. The world was divided between those who were Christians and those who weren't. God loved everybody but in order to be with him, people had to make decisions like I had and become like me and my friends. I always struggled with the concept of condemnation but, as it seemed a clear teaching of the Bible, I accepted it.

With my husband, I started to work in a foreign country but still in the context of the Christian churches. I was happy to see that we could help a few people to discover a loving God instead of the strict judge they seemed to know. We tried to show our friends in the churches that everybody can find a way towards and with God - that it is not the job of a pastor or priest to do that for others. We tried to show God's love to needy people around us and tried to encourage others to follow our example. At that time I noticed a change of climate in our church. Little by little it got decidedly colder and, over the months, (and with just a few exceptions) it even grew hostile towards us.

That was a time when I started to have a lot of questions again. I had grown used to reading the bible, prayer, study and was turning around in circles. Deep in my heart was the question, "Is this all? Is there nothing more to discover? Is God so small, so boring?"

Whilst the opposition to our positive approach towards people outside of the churches grew stronger, I started looking for something else. Not knowing what the 'something else was' I began to surf the internet for spiritual alternatives. That year, I got drawn to Brighid and felt very guilty for my feelings. Something happened in my heart and I started to write poetry to express some of the feelings that were welling up. Then one day, while browsing the internet, I found the website of the Céile Dé and it felt like a coming home to a barely remembered past. The more I learned, the more I realised that God was showing me a new way forward and helping me to open up to the light I'd discovered in my heart. I was overjoyed to find out that this God, who seemed so small just a little while before, was so much bigger than I had thought possible - so much closer than I had dared to wish - so much happier, loving, caring than I could imagine. Suddenly the whole world became the image of God and my home, my kin. New insights multiplied and I was so glad to see that there would be new things to learn for the rest of my life...

Spending time with God, just listening and being there made me reconnect with the land I lived in, feel close to all creatures around me. I found a light in my heart that hasn't stopped growing since, and that nurtures and sustains me, even though times have been quite rough otherwise. Every day has become a new adventure and the calm in my heart and soul carries me through the difficult times we had when the differences between us and a group in our church came to a head last year. I am walking forward and inwards at the same time, slowly but surely. Who knows what is waiting for me round the next bend?

My Soul

*My soul is a mirror, reflecting your image*
*My soul is a sponge, absorbing your love*
*My soul is a candle, burning quietly*
*My soul is a falcon, flying high*
*My soul is a swallow, sailing on the breeze*
*My soul is an eagle, soaring heavenwards*
*My soul is a wolf, prowling in the dark*
*My soul is a lion, tracking its prey*
*My soul is a bear, eating honey*
*My soul is a river, filling his bed*
*My soul is a creek, dancing over rocks*
*My soul is the ocean, ebbing, flowing*
*My soul is a cloud, moving slowly*
*My soul is a shadow, following your movements*
*My soul is twilight, time between times*
*My soul is ever growing, expanding, reaching beyond*
*Feeding from love, through her roots,*
*Drinking deeply from the well of the heart*

Marion describes herself as 'a relative newcomer to the Ceile De' and, with that in mind wants her words to be seen as a personal contribution and not representative of everyone in the Ceile De. She is a nurse from the south of Scotland?

## Marion's Story

My spiritual background is in Protestant Christianity. I was brought up in the Church of Scotland by parents who were originally Baptist and Congregational, but had reservations about how much of the creed they believed. They brought me up to love nature as God's creation, and that the basis of Christianity is Love.

I became a 'born again Christian' at the age of 15, whilst attending an evangelical youth camp. Questions I had about the church and God seemed to be answered by a revelation that it was a living Jesus that it was all about. I took this to mean that I should do what the leaders asked, and give my life to this Jesus. I had many years in evangelical churches, and found a lot of love, support, wisdom and friendship. I was baptised by full immersion to show my devotion to Jesus. I took part in the music of the church and church groups. Outwardly I agreed with the evangelical creed that said Jesus died on the cross for my sin and, because I believe in Him I have eternal life. However inwardly I saw God as loving and forgiving whether or not we are born-again Christians. I didn't believe He could be so narrow minded as to exclude people who see things differently.

Gradually I realised I was living a lie, so I left the church. At first I felt isolated and alone. If church wasn't for me, then what was? I realised it might be a long time before I would find any sort of answer.

I explored Justice and Environmental groups, Reiki, a 12-step programme, meditation, Buddhist and Indian spirituality, all of which I found helpful and nourishing. But I felt there was a need to include nature and the seasons in my spirituality, and yet I still wanted to retain my basic belief of love being at the centre of life and spirituality. I also felt there should be a home-grown spirituality. Why should we have to go to Tibet, India or even Israel for guidance in the inner life? I liked the idea of the 'Old Religion' I had read about in Marion Bradley's Avalon books, but thought it was long dead. I read about the Ceile De in a brochure of the premises they were using for meetings. Evidently a Celtic form of spirituality was still alive!! I went to a meeting and, as I listened, entranced, it became apparent that all the strands I had held important through the years were combined in this ancient, very wise and balanced tradition. My fractured self could find unity at last!

So as I meditate in this tradition, I open myself to the love of Heaven and Earth.

Wise teachings include the use of myths which are flexible in interpretation, not set in stone. They draw on the wisdom and love of countless generations of Celtic people over the centuries.

I am learning Gaelic songs and prayers (but God understands English too!). The songs express love, longing, faith, dedication, gratitude, in tunes inspired by nature and weather and which come from the heart.

I feel I have come home. The Ceile De tradition brings together so many parts of my makeup that it feels like I am becoming a whole person for the first time! It combines love of God with love of the Land. In fact the Land is part of God - life is a whole, not separated into physical, mental and spiritual. It sees spiritual growth as vital, fed by myth, and guidance from a soul friend. It combines mysticism with deep understanding of the human psyche. And it comes from the lands of the Gael, a home-grown spirituality that speaks to the poetic Celtic soul like no other religion could! The music of the tradition - sacred songs - grew from the sounds of nature and the weather, expressed with the longing, hope and courage of Gaelic bards. The simple words are heartfelt prayers which the music gives wings to. I find it amazing and am so grateful that we are beneficiaries of the learning and wisdom of 'spouses of God' through 20 centuries, the first of who realised we could have a loving relationship with the Divine even before they heard of Jesus the Christ.

# Chapter 17

# Christo-Druids

*For a Druid Christian, the Earth and all creation is an expression of the deity as presence, and therefore deeply sacred. While there are Christians who acknowledge this without moving into Druidry, others find that the philosophies significantly strengthen and broaden their faith. Deepening the acceptance, within the framework of Christianity, of the power and beauty of the divine gift of the physical, there is opened up also the respect for sexuality, for birth, our genetic inheritance, and with it reverence for our ancestors. The Earth, its flora and fauna, humanity and all creation become an altar to God. In an age when environmentalism, the importance of family and community, interest in folk traditions and natural medicine, are all increasing, the point at which Druidry and Christianity meet becomes clearer.*
Emma Restall-Orr[67]

Barbara Erskine is a best-selling author of the most remarkable historical fiction. Her novels are passionate, gripping, highly convincing and quite magical. She is also a wise woman who manages, beautifully, to walk the road between the two worlds of Christianity and Druidry.

## Barbara's Story
When I was a child I set up an altar in woodland at the bottom of the garden. On it I put a little gold cross-wedged into a lump of plasticine. Now, many years later, I realise this was a first expression of leanings towards what I now recognise as druidic Christianity, or Christian Druidism.

I came from a Church of England family and went to a school

which worshipped daily in the chapel. Faith foundered however when I studied history at university. I encountered for the first time Christianity's downside: it had been too much mediated by politics, cruelty, misogyny and fundamentalism, caring little for Jesus' teachings of tolerance and love; it seemed to encourage exploitation of the natural world and it used the heavy hand of guilt rather than love to corral its followers. Like many others I questioned and fell away.

When I discovered Druidry it was a homecoming into a philosophy which encompassed all that I held dear and it brought me into the western spiritual tradition, something which had been part of my soul without my realising it. My world was animistic. I had always prayed to the one God and all the gods, feeling that that expressed my true beliefs even though I was not comfortable with wholesale paganism. The last thing I expected was for my studies and meditations to illumine and rekindle my struggling Christian faith. Or that they would reconcile my certainties about a supernatural world of nature spirits, ghosts and energies which seemed to be unchristian, into a church which included angels and archangels and all the company of heaven.

Druidry acted as a change of focus; a personal reinterpretation; an altered attitude. It shone a beam of light into a monochrome landscape and reminded me of an ancient church where Celtic saints had called blessings onto rain-soaked hills, where St Kevin allowed a blackbird to nest on his hand, where Brighid was both goddess and saint, a church where Our Lady was also the Star of the Sea, a blessed feminine warmth which a more puritan faith had distanced. Ancient prayers took on deeper meanings for me. Now the Benedicite read like a Celtic hymn. The druidical circle of seasons was there within the liturgy, sacred geometry was there, though forgotten by most, as were the healing energies of stone and stained glass and the mysticism of ancient words.

Historians and theologians may find the belief untenable but I like the idea of long-ago druids segueing neatly with the changing focus of the heavens into a Celtic Christianity. It feels right.

My practice of meditation evolved naturally back into one of regular prayer and though prayer can happen every and anywhere I set up a small altar of my own again. In its centre I have a beautiful statue made by a friend, of the Blessed Virgin, not a meek, mild obedient role model, but Queen of Heaven, with crown and royal robes. On her knee is the Christ child. At the four corners of the altar I have put symbols of earth air fire and water. There is a Celtic cross there, and flowers. Sometimes I have incense. Sometimes meditation oils. Sometimes this is the centre of my druid rituals. I use it as a place to pray, to meditate and to listen. Unorthodox? Probably. But it makes perfect sense to me.'[68]

Sébastien Beaudoin is an Artist, Potter and Druid (RDNA). As well as being a Druid he is a Christian, and finds the two spiritual paths to be complimentary rather than incompatible. He lives in Quebec, Canada. For more information on Sébastien's work please visit www.atelierdudruide.com

## Christo-Druidry a living spirituality

To ask me how I became a druid is like asking me why a bird can fly? Birds do it by nature. Mostly, a bird knows it can truly fly when it takes it's first leap of faith and jumps out of its nest. But there are also some birds that discover they can fly at the defining moment when they accidentally fall out! I am like that last bird; I fell unto the path of Druidry by own misfortune... or was it? Was druidry truly hidden in my own nature? I strongly believe that we were sent here to experience life, and that we each have a soul purpose and calling.

In becoming a Druid, I decided to also keep my Christian heritage and not deny it like so many do, or will do, on their druidic path. When I became a Druid, I did not embark on my journey as an act of rebellion or as an act of disgust towards religion. Thanks to many circumstances, I have discovered that I am able to mix both my Christian faith and my Druidry. It is not always easy, but I have discovered that it was always in my nature to do so, therefore impossible to ignore or repress.

I know that some will argue that one cannot be a Christian and a Druid. But my answer to that is I do exist and I do mix very well together both traditions. I discovered that one could keep his Christian tradition and still hold nature in reverence and practice Druidry. If one really looks deeply within this concept, one will easily understand that a Christian Druid can easily identify the immanence of God within nature and easily practice Druidry. Personally, my Druid practices and my reverence for nature have both deepened my faith and brought me closer to God. I find that in Christian Druidry, nature and all its wonders provide us the key not just to establish the existence of God but also in finding out more about his presence in our world, his presence in the soft wind over a field of wheat, in the loud growling thunder of a storm cloud, in the flight of geese over head or in the shiny little trout in the swirling pool of a clear brook.

As a Christian Druid, my theology is very down to earth and levelheaded. It seems very obvious to me that if you are in touch with creation, then you are in touch with the Creator. For me to rebut Christianity was not the answer to what I was looking for and did not fit into my personal ethics and values. For me to believe in a multitude of gods and goddesses or to believe just in one does not make any difference in my own Druidry. I believe that once you become a Druid, a great doorway of knowledge and understanding opens up to you, you begin to see a world hidden that you have never seen or experienced, you start to observe, experience and feel that you belong to whole new world, a world in constant transformation and mutation, that all is sacred and interconnected to one great central force that I call the source of all creation. Today my druidry is deeply enriched by a combination of many spiritual traditions but mainly it has become an interweaving Christian and druidic tapestry. I believe that, in Druidry, no one is obligated in denying their upbringing, their family nor their heritage and culture, in fact no one should!

Honestly, it is wonderful to be open to all religions and faiths. It has permitted me to straightforwardly continue my studies in Druidry and follow my path while I'm always centered within myself and within God. In my opinion, what characterizes a Christian Druid is his love of learning and wisdom, his reverence of Nature, his respect of the ancestors and his fellowship with Christ in his own way. I personally took the best from the old tradition while still keeping in touch with Christ within me. Today, I attend my own chapel under the sky, amongst the animals, the natural elements and plants. My Chapel is found right in the middle of God's creation. It is there where I can meet

God in person and alone in prayer.

In a sense the goal of a Christian Druid isn't to be more religious, but to be more alive, more awake and sensitive to the divinity pulsing throughout the universe. Did I truly fall unto the path of Druidry, or was it in my nature? One thing for sure, it has become my devotion and my calling.

My life journey has always been a long and winding stream, knowing one day that I will find my way to the sea.

What is Druidry?
*It is setting out on a journey*
*Only yourself can walk*
*In contact with Earth*
*In contact with self*
*Aware of the Sacredness*
*And the world around you*
*Working within Nature*
*Within Nature's Laws*
*Deeply involved*
*Deep within the sacred cycles*
*Life's Fertility,*
*Life's abundance and perpetuity*
*Birth, death and rebirth*
*Speaking to the Sacred*
*Speaking to the ancients*
*Speaking straightforwardly to land*
*With truth, loyalty, trust, hospitality and honor*
*Always listening and deciphering the messages*
*Hearing the voices beyond words*
*Powered by will and intent*
*Empowered by deep intuition*
*The gift of insight*
*Of knowledge and learning*
*Perception and vision*

*Walking with and within*
*Shaped by my own muse*
*Having a presence*
*And assuming it.*

Rt. Revd. Alistair Bate is a fascinating man. Once a Unitarian Minister he now serves as a Bishop of the Independent Liberal Catholic Church. He is also a Druid and founded the Christian Druid Trinity Grove, based in Edinburgh.

## The Oak and the Cross

I have been a Christian all my life and a member of a modern Druid Order for nearly ten years, though my interest in Druidism began in childhood. Throughout the years I have tried to hold my Druidism and Christianity in a creative tension, but it would be true to say that my primary identity is undoubtedly as a Christian and a Bishop and I would put my identity as a Druid on a par with my identity as a Freemason, a Templar, and a Theosophist; membership of each of these orders being supplementary and complementary to my primary Christian identity. The same would be true for most Christian Druids of the last three centuries, whilst for the 21st century neo-Pagan Druid, on the other hand, simply being a Druid has become a primary religious identity, in a way which was unheard of this side of the early dark ages. Does this mean that the neo-Pagan Druid has a greater claim to authenticity? This may not necessarily be the case. Perhaps the Christian Druid is simply more in touch with the bigger esoteric picture. As a Pagan friend of mine once said about a Christian Druid of her acquaintance "I used to think that X was confused until I realised that he is just very knowledgeable!"

To many in our society the word "pagan" is still confused with the word "atheist" and it is an enlightening moment when someone discovers Paganism as an alternative religion, however, in my opinion Paganism is often just as much rooted in secularism as it is in alternative theology for it includes under its umbrella scientific pantheists and even humanists as well as people of other theological persuasions. Regrettably, in my experience there is still something counter-cultural and specifically anti-Christian about many neo-pagans.

The gradual dawning of the rationalist enlightenment has exposed the foundational Christian myths for what they are, myths and, sadly, many in the pulpits and in the pews have not understood the value and power of myth and have thrown out the baby with the bath-water, reducing Christianity to little more than a few morality tales. Positively, neo-pagan Druidry is an attempt to re-present some ancient myths is a way more suitable and reasonable for our times. Lives that have worth and meaning are lives lived with a sense of wonder and positive anticipation and the re-mythologising and re-enchantment promoted by druidry are definitely one means of filling that need for some people. Where I may differ as a Christian Druid is that I find in Celtic and esoteric Christianity, as well as pre-neo-pagan fraternal and cultural Druidism, a blend of Christian and pre-Christian myth and magic, experienced as one system when seen as different aspects of the Western Mystery tradition. To wrench the Christian mythos, which has been so formative of our spirituality and culture, from the heart of Celtic spirituality, for example, in order to present a Druidry, shorn of Christian influence, would be a grave mistake, for to the true Celtic soul, the Christian and pre-Christian myths are so intertwined, interdependent and complementary as to be inseparable.

When a Christian, who has had problems with the negative side of institutionalised religion discovers the vibrant freedom and charm of Druidry there is often a great sense of relief and a casting aside of forms of worship previously held precious. But for many of us the new/old spirituality is found in time to be not quite so profound as we hoped and we turn back to the tradition of our birth to reconnect with the central themes of incarnation, crucifixion, resurrection and ascension with a renewed appreciation and understanding. I would certainly never regret the few years in which I identified as a Pagan for I firmly believe that neo-Paganism has enabled me to understand and appreciate the central themes of Christianity more deeply.

As a Theosophist I can also understand the various traditions in which I work as representative of different rays or paths. I see Christian religious devotion as working on the Red or 6th ray, magical and ceremonial work in the esoteric tradition as working on the Violet or 7th ray and working with Druidry and Shamanism as work on the Green or 3rd ray, though each of these disciplines may include work on secondary and tertiary rays as well as on their primary ray.

People like to fit spirituality into neat little boxes labeled "Christian", "Pagan", "Buddhist" or whatever. Maybe "Eclectic" or even "Universalist" are just two more labels. If so, so be it. Here I stand, firmly in the Universalist tradition of Druidry founded in the early 20th century by George Watson MacGregor Reid; firmly with the Theosophists who uphold the Society's motto "There is no religion higher than truth" and firmly with the one of the founders of my own Liberal Catholic tradition, Bishop Leadbeater, who was amongst the first Church leaders to teach that there are many paths up the same mountain.

So, for some of us, the oak is the cross of Esus, a foreshadowing of Christ among the ancient Celts. It may also be the World Tree of Odin, whence he hung to obtain wisdom and bring liberation and the Cross is the cross of the four directions, the four beasts of revelation, the four alchemical elements of the Druid circle, the four evangelists and archangels. The Oak and the Cross are so interconnected and entwined as to be inseparable and to attempt a separation is to diminish the other. May the religion of the future recognise that our myths are mirrors of each other and, for those with the eyes to see, all reflect the one Divine Unity.[69]

Álvaro Herrera (Aelfarh) is a Celtic-Christo-Pagan in the spirit, a Music Composer in his heart and a Mechanical Engineer in his mind. He came from a Catholic background and even when not practicing any more, he finds the teachings of Jesus Christ enlightening and complementary to his spiritual path. He was born in Mexico City and currently lives in London, UK. You can visit his blog in English at http://al-tirnanog.blogspot.com/ and his Spanish language website on Druidry at www.losceltas.org

## Álvaro's Story

Many years have passed since I began this journey. It began back in 1991 when, thanks to a great singer and composer named Enya, I discovered the Celtic culture. In those days, only a boy, I started searching for facts about this fascinating people, somehow misunderstood by many.

This journey of mine - my infatuation with the Celts - has not ended and every single day I find that there's more and more to learn. It's been not just a journey of knowledge. In many ways it's been a journey of self-discovery.

This path leads me closer to my origins and, also to the ancient pagan world in general - from Rome to the Celtic lands, from the Mayan realm to the Aztec Empire. Those ancient roots that are part of me and, in many ways, are part of humankind itself. It has maybe lead me a little distance from the earliest catholic ways I was educated within, but since they are also part of my life, I do not renounce those roots completely. I just find that there's not only one true religion or true point of view but, instead, there is Truth which could be approached in many, many ways.

Some hold that it's impossible and incompatible to believe in both Pagan and Christian ways. If you're a fundamentalist, it could be. On the other hand I'm not searching for the conflict, I'm searching of the common ground. Christianity, in its roots, is a religion of love, respect, and tolerance, which worships the

Creator of all things - the first principle and the last end, as Plato defined Him. But after years of Christendom it has been contaminated by politics, cruelty, power, misogyny and fundamentalism, caring little for Jesus' teachings of tolerance and love. However, politics apart, the Christian teachings have a great hollow - everything is human based and there is the imagery of the earth as something entrusted to us, separated from us. And that's where some pagan teaching come along. Studying Celtic culture and spirituality, I discovered the beauty and importance of all living, and not living things. The Celts were people that live next to the nature. Trees were sacred, so were animals and stones. Earth, Sky and Sea, the trinity of creation on this world ruled their lives. They were also believers in three basic principles, Wisdom, Creativity and Love; and have three basics for their ethics, Truth in our hearts, strength in our arms, and fulfilment in our tongues. During this search I found that, if you know where to look, you will see and feel the power of these spirits, these forces of nature, this Tuatha Dé Danann, these children of Danu or the Goddess mother, the earth itself.

They are forces that (at the same time) are and are not part of this world - our ancestors, our elders, or maybe our big brothers and sisters (as I call them). We all are divine and sacred, since we all were created by the same Great Spirit and Force. And it is neither male nor female, because it's far away of these earthly attributes. Knowing, understanding, believing, feeling, dreaming of all this, is how my journey leads me to many ways, to the old ways, lost in the centuries.

Throughout this searching of my inner self, I could not ignore the ancient pagan ways of the two main civilizations that lived in what is now Mexico, my native country. Mayans and Aztecs are part of my culture. Great wisdom also comes to me from sources like Popol-vuh and Chilam Balam.

But even when I learn a lot But even when I learn a lot from these cultures, so too from Greek and from Greek and Roman pagan teachings, this fascination, this infatuation with the Celtic culture is much stronger. It's something that can't be explained in words, a passion that emerges whenever I read about them, listen to their music, or now, walk in their lands. Some call this Henotheism, in this modern way of putting a name or label to everything, but I'm not comfortable with stereotypes or labels.

Sixteen years later, destiny put on my path the opportunity to walk and live in a Celtic land. I'm now living in Sussex, England and in just a few months of being here I have learned more than in all those years - but not learning data, names or legends, the learning has been completely for my spirit. Walking through sacred places, breathing the cold air and listening to the old sea.

I have not renounced Christ. For me the lessons of Jesus' life are alive and are valid still. I just open myself to other realities, to other possibilities and neglect the concepts of intolerance that some (and I'll mark my words, 'some') Christian Churches and individuals hold.

Chapter 18

# Pagan Druids

*For me, Druidry is an exuberant celebration of nature's currents, its tides and cycles, an intense journey of exploration and discovery in natural science and emotion. It is about the wild energy of being alive and breathing deeply, right where life shimmers and shudders with its own awareness: in the throes of change, collapse, dying, birthing, waking. It is about the stillness in the pause between ebb and flow. Druidry is about finding the beauty of it, all of it, consciously, wherever we are, in the tranquillity of isolation and in the chattering clutter of the crowd. It is far from a way of seeing or living that could be called conventional. Furthermore, for me, that consciousness is coloured, too, with more than a splash of eleventh percent perception.*
Emma Restall Orr[70]

Hans C Kamerman (Katsu). Hans is a Manager with a large retail company, in the Netherlands. He is also a forum supervisor on the website forum of The Order of Bards, Ovates and Druids.

### Mabon/Alban Elfed - *Light of the Water* [71]
Some years ago.....this tale begins. 'T was my parents 5th wedding anniversary and, though I was expected several days before, my dad was sure; "He'll be here on our wedding day". He got it right... but little did I recognise that day's significance, till about 20 years later.

I grew up as a dutiful Christian, going to a Church (Protestant) School.

At the age of 10 I woke one night and asked the Divine to

show It (Him/Her) self to me. I understand my arrogance now in doing so, but It non-the-less granted my request.

At the age of 11, we had the opportunity to declare our faith in Church. So I did.

At the age of 18 we had the opportunity to be baptised again (for lack of a better word…..) I had become a full member of the Church. And I continued to work within the Church; even teaching the Bible to 12/13 yr olds.

Yet one thing bothered me - no one could answer certain questions… especially 'Why?' The one question everyone was avoiding was 'Why?' If asked why floods happened or why wars and massacres occurred there were no answers, just lots of dogmatic responses.

I left home for University and studied Japanese Language and Culture. The College was multi-religious / multicultural, so at last I discovered different faiths - Shinto, Buddhism, Paganism etc. It felt somewhat like coming home but not quite.

I studied more and more nature based Faiths, some of which I found were also into Dogma. I desired none.

Then, one day, a friend of mine (whom I will love for that till time's end) introduced me to the Druid's Path. He showed me a Path that helped me find my own perception of Deity - a personal one, a Force, yet not a name. This deity was a Being, both male/female - my true Anam Cara (Soul friend), God and Goddess alike.

Through this friend, I've founds other friends whom I hold very dear. A Seedgroup[71] has been a result of this. Later this year I'll perform a ritual of Handfasting of two of my closest friends. And I've been working for our Druid Organisation (aka the OBOD) for a few years now as Moderator on the website.

So that leaves me, still the same person, just with a different perception of Deity.

Rhonda Rawlins (WillowCat). Rhonda lives in Danville, Virginia, USA and works for the State of VA, Division of Child Support Enforcement.

## Rhonda's Story

I was raised in both the Catholic and Episcopal Churches, eventually settling in the Episcopal Church. But from the beginning I had problems with the doctrine. I tended towards depression, due to a low self-image (which I have fortunately overcome), and I found the attitude that I was barely worthy of notice, that I had to beg for attention and forgiveness, difficult to deal with. I frequently left the services feeling depressed instead of inspired (as I was told I should feel). I could not help but wonder what I was doing wrong.

As time passed, I also began to notice an US versus THEM mentality which I did not like. I also was unhappy with some of the attitudes towards women, that she (I) should be submissive to a male - that women were somehow less worthy.

By time I reached my mid 40's I had left the church feeling I just did not fit in, but I felt adrift....in a something of a spiritual void. However, with access to the internet, I began to do some research on alternative spiritualities and eventually came across Druidry. Its basis in the natural rhythms of life and the open-minded attitude of the members really spoke to me. The more I learned of it, the more I embraced it.

Since I've experienced my "spiritual renewal" I've become much more satisfied with life.... and even felt free to explore facets of myself that I either never knew or had forgotten. I've begun to write again - something I've not done for 15 or 20 years. I've also discovered I have a talent for oil painting (and I would NEVER have thought I'd be an artist!). I am much more aware of the natural world around me and find myself amazed at how much beauty I've overlooked. I make it a point to 'stop and smell the roses' on a regular basis.

I still have the greatest respect for those who get something from traditional Christianity and organized religion, but it just did not work for me. I now have my own, very personal and satisfying, relationship with my gods. (That is another thing, I always felt the idea of a single male deity somehow incomplete. I now honor a male and female pairing which seems so much more right to me.)

It's been a long journey, with a few wrong turns here and there, but a wonderful learning experience and now that I feel I'm on the right path, I find I enjoy the ride even more.

Danielle, a mother from Boise Idaho, training herself on the path of an Ovate (second grade of The Order of Bards, Ovates and Druids. See Danielle's own story for a brief description of what Ovate means).

## Danielle's story.

Finding Druidry was amazing. It felt like coming home. All my life I felt like I didn't fit in anywhere; work, school, home, family. I always felt 'different'. I worked hard to be a good Catholic, to please the Father, to please my mother. I fasted, made rosaries, went to daily mass, said a couple 52-day novenas, and always held a special devotion to the Blessed Mother. But it often felt like my life was being lived in a tumble-dryer, helplessly in the control of some external being that I could not predict, understand or seem to make peace with.

The crumbling of the traditional Christian faith started three years ago when we tried to adopt a child and after a year of misery and stress, it all fell apart. We were blessed with a conceived child, but I couldn't help but wonder why a "God" who tells us to care for the widows and children, would keep one child in an orphanage and bring a new child into an already crowded world. (And make a struggling couple loose $20,000 in the process).

Over the course of two years the discrepancy between what I was taught about this "Father-God" and what I saw in the world became more and more obvious, until I could no longer reconcile the paradigm of "God".

Meanwhile I walked in the living room one evening where my husband was watching a show with women singing, and it quite literally stopped me in my tracks. I am not a television watcher, but at that moment whatever I had been doing was instantly forgotten and I was transfixed. It was a live performance of "The Celtic Woman' in Ireland. This led me to buy the CD and, wanting to learn all the songs, I began to learn basic Gaelic.

One of the songs lyrics are "The Druids lived here once, they say. Forgotten is the race that no one knows." Druids? It sounded faintly familiar, but who, or what, were Druids? And so, following that thread that led me on my journey:  I googled, I surfed, I read, chatted and learned. And in doing so I stepped off the path of religious 'undecided' onto the path of paganism: NeoDruidry.

Here was a place that made sense of my eclectic abundance of talents and interests: gardening, herbology, natural healing, intuitive/emotional healing, art and music of all sorts, Earth-friendly living, languages, writing, dancing, history. Through my studies of Druidry I suddenly realized that I DID have a place in the world; I was not alone in thinking as I did. What had, until now, seemed a random, scattered assortment of interests that only categorized me as 'odd' in the world, actually fit into two beautiful, simple explanations: Bard and Ovate.

The Bard - the historian, the artist, the teacher.

The Ovate - the scientist and the healer and the master of nature.

I completely understand the world though a relationship with the non-personified deity I refer to as the "great divine", or "Awen" when I pray. The inconsistencies of a humanistic God who does not think or act like a human are gone.  I understand life as I am part of it here on Earth, rather than pining away for a life hereafter, and can celebrate the cycles of nature as they reflect the cycles in our own lives. I pray to connect myself with a divine who is part of me, rather than an external being, and I cherish the appreciation of balance in all things.

I find that with Druidry I am free to express my artistic and literary visions as a form of respect and glory in themselves, without them being scruitinized by restrictive standards (I started covertly writing historical romance novels several years ago - 'naughty', 'dirty' books that they are!), and without them being metamorphasized into symbolism for the life of Jesus. The more I study paganism and druidry, the more I realize that Christianity is a step back from Judaism, toward their pagan roots. Judaism is strict monotheistic with no goddess-figure, but Catholicism has bridged that in the form of the trinity, and the non-deified Blessed Mother. Christians took the symbols and the gods of the pagans and attached their own meanings to them, so that I never quite could relate to the symbols. Evergreen trees, eggs, holly, in the pagan context, not only make sense, but hold very deep meaning. The only challenge is being a desert-dweller in America with symbols that occur in the cool, damp climates on the other half of the globe! There is some modification and individualization that must occur to make it meaningful at times. I have just come to accept this about myself. My journey is still very young - a child who has just learned to crawl and is exploring the world on a level very close to the earth. I have just made a big step in my bardic journey: my first public performance, as a belly dancer (to Celtic music!), thus overcoming my apprehensions about performing in public. I will admit I have a long road ahead of me, but at least I feel that this time I am on the right path.

Rob Draper (Badger Bob). Bob lives in The Peak District UK. He describes himself as a 'mathemagician'.

## Bob's Story

A decade ago I decided to look into Christianity as a possible path for me to follow. I had been a spiritual tourist for many years living in Buddhist communities and being more or less Pagan since the early eighties when I discovered Druidry through an advert in the back of Prediction magazine. I decided to ignore my problems with the church and just see if I could be Christian. I had been brought up as a Christian but the happy-clappy element had made me uncomfortable about being anywhere near a church, even though I have always loved the history of the Church in England and the artistic aspects of it all. The cathedrals, the stained glass and the wonderful music of the likes of Tallis and Byrd had always fascinated and comforted me even though I had no particular love of the driving force behind them. Eventually I started to attend a mid-high Anglican service at my local cathedral and ended up being talked into confirmation after a year or so. I had always had nagging doubts about my motivation though, I love the smells and bells approach and I enjoy my hour or so of meditative time on a Sunday morning but I still have problems with God.

My main objections fall squarely into two related areas, the problem of the two natures of God between the Old and New Testaments and the problem of eternal damnation. Tertullian does nothing to convince me that the God of the OT is the same as the God of the NT, I have always been with Marcion on that score. The sheer difference in the tone of the OT from the loving father of the NT has always been my sticking point, if I could reject the OT entirely and still be Christian then I would be, but when I mentioned that to a bishop he simply laughed and told me that it was an all or nothing problem. There is much in the OT that I hate, the treatment of the Egyptians in Exodus, the treatment of the Canaanites who have their land pinched by God's chosen people (God never gave the Canaanites a chance as far as I can see) and the wholesale slaughter sanctioned by God in defiance of his own commandment led me to find the OT to be one of the most vile pieces of writing I have ever encountered. In contrast to that I still find the NT to be a beautiful and inspiring book, showing us how we should behave towards each other. While I have my doubts about some of the writings attributed to Paul I find books such as the Gospel of John to be wonderful in their execution and intent. This is how I ache for Christianity to be, but from bitter experience the taint of OT conservatism is to be found just about everywhere.

Currently I am pretty much back to my pagan roots, I still flick through the NT from time to time but I prefer to see Christ as an exemplary human being (Marcionite and Arian - I can almost smell the burning torches!) or maybe even an avatar of a sun-god, who showed us a way of dealing with our fellows with extraordinary love, patience and forgiveness and who should be imitated as far as possible. As for God, I prefer to see God in the multitude of Celtic, Norse and other archetypal Gods and Goddesses that I find through Druidry, Jesus and Mary included where their specific archetypes are appropriate. I also abhor the idea of a final judgement without any way to redeem oneself in this life or the next other than by trusting to the saviour-figure. Justification by works seems to be the only way that a sane God could operate - justification by faith alone opens the door to a whole host of unsavoury practices in the name of God. For me, the end of life sees a natural judgement process and an entry into another realm (or maybe back here) where we lead another finite, mortal life and so on for eternity. Infinite punishment for a single finite lifetime of sin would be the wholly unjust action of a psychopathic supreme being. As Gilbert & Sullivan said, let the punishment fit the crime.

Matthew Long (Fiach MacMara). Matthew Long was born in Hannibal, Missouri, USA. He has served as a sailor in U.S. Navy for past 8 years. He works on submarines. He was once a catholic monk

## Matthew's Story

My introduction to spirituality and religion came as a child. I was raised in a devout Catholic home and was encouraged from a very young age to consider a vocation to the priesthood or religious life. Everything about church came very easily to me. I was a spiritual person and I loved the intimacy of my relationship with god. For me faith and belief were not intertwined with the Catechism or even with the Bible. They were independent entities which existed in the personal relationship between me and the divine.

I spent some time in a boarding school for boys while in high school and we were focused on developing our vocation to the priesthood. It was a positive and formative period in my life but it also introduced me to some of the legalistic aspects of the Catholic Church. While there I realized that I could not be a parish priest but that I still wanted to develop my spirituality in that one on one relationship with god. I entered a Benedictine monastery and spent a couple years there. Truly this was one of the most rewarding times in my life.

Looking back I realize that I did not necessarily believe in and worship god in the same way that most Catholics do. For me it was not so much about Jesus and the crucifixion and salvation history. For me, the relationship with the divine was about creation and joy, celebrating the life of the earth and all it contained. I eventually left the monastery and the Catholic Church due to a phenomenon that I term Catholic guilt. It was an aspect of the life of the church that I didn't enjoy and didn't believe had a legitimate place in the spiritual lives of people. I personally held no ill will towards the church and the vast majority of my family are still practicing Catholics. I value and appreciate the lessons I received and the moral background that was instilled in me as a result of my Christian upbringing. I believe that the Bible is one of the great spiritual books of history. I don't read it as factual. I read the bible as a collection of stories and morals; a guide for how to live our lives as good people.

About eight or ten years ago I began searching for an alternative spiritual path that was more in line with my personal ideas about how we experience god or what I call the Divine Experience. The biggest pieces of this are some tenants that have developed into my personal credo:

- the Divine is all encompassing. It exists in all things and in all places and in all times.
- we can experience the Divine in a personal and intimate relationship.
- our experience of the Divine can come in many forms. We can see it as a single divine entity or as many manifestations. This is most evident in our experiences of the gods of places (i.e. rivers and forest).
- there is a life beyond this one. Its true nature is a mystery except to those who have been given the gift to see the other side.
- Our responsibility in this life is to do the right thing. Live a good life, be a good person. There are no rules which save us or condemn us. Our internal moral compass is our guide. Every person knows right from wrong.

These basic ideas took some time to form for me but eventually they led to an interest in nature spiritualities. I have always believed that my experience of the Divine was strongest when I was close to creation. So I began to seek out information about different nature paths.

Eventually I stumbled upon Druidry. I found the website of OBOD and registered. After reading through many of the posts and also a lot of the information on the general website I decided to join the Order. About the same time I found the Ancient Order of Druid's in America (AODA). I also joined them as the two groups have a good working relationship and there is no conflict in their instruction. I am currently working through the Bard grade of the OBOD course and I am a Druid Candidate in AODA.

I like these groups because they do not preach to you and tell you what you can and cannot believe. For me this is the most vital and important part of a spiritual journey. Our relationship with the Divine is an intensely personal one and each journey should have the freedom to develop in its own uniqueness. Within the confines of an organized religion this is sometimes not an easy option.

I also believe that there is a place for magic and mystery within the confines of a spiritual tradition. While I have no skills or talents in these areas they are things that I am deeply fascinated by and interested in. The arts of alchemy and divination hold a great deal of treasure for those who are willing to pursue those paths.

In this past year since I began my formal studies I have found such a tremendous amount of growth and peace within myself. I am closer now to the Divine than I have ever been. I think also that I am a better person as I am actively seeking to live a better life.

I think it is important for people to have peace in their soul with regards to all of their lives experiences and for me the Christian journey that was at the beginning of my life was a rewarding one in which the foundation was established for a really rewarding spiritual life. While I don't consider myself a Christian any longer it is not a negative experience in my life and

I bode no ill will towards those who do follow that path. Each path is unique and wherever we are most able to find god then it is there that we should dwell.

Jinny Peberday (Moonhare) is a psychotherapist nearing the end of her (very long) training. She lives near Bristol with one black and one white cat. Current obsessions include knitting, drop spinning and watching the sky change.

## Jinny's Story

As I write this in late August, part of my garden is still ablaze with marigolds. I scattered the seeds over the earth earlier this spring and left them to take their chances. I collected them over four years ago, from a convent garden. I'd gone on an eight-day silent retreat in what was really a last-ditch attempt to hang onto my Christian faith. During the retreat I spent hours walking in the surrounding countryside and helping with the Sisters' garden – every morning I ignored the bells for Lauds and went instead to the tool shed. I spent a good couple of hours before breakfast digging out the tenacious roots of ground elder. Later in the day I would do some gentler weeding and dead-heading. I tried to pray with the Stations of the Cross, to take communion, to agree that I needed to go to church every Sunday – but I couldn't do it. It had all become physically and emotionally repellent. When I got home I had to admit to myself that none of this meant anything to me. It has been a gradual dissolution and a painful one. For me loss of faith also meant a loss of identity.

At twelve I became a born again Christian and spent many summers involved with children's missions and was president of the school Christian union (an activity that won me few friends!). At university I studied theology with the aim of entering ordained ministry or of entering a convent and spending my life as an Anglican Religious (the correct term for "nun"). I became involved in Christian groups, street evangelism and went to church meetings of one sort or another nearly everyday. But I think already the cracks were beginning to appear in what I thought was a solid faith. I remember beginning to question things – such as, how can an all-loving God sanction the existence of hell? Voicing this led to a swift visit from the Christian Union president. He wouldn't even cross the threshold but stood outside and told me that "hell is endless pain and suffering and it is eternal." Full stop.

For many reasons, I became neither a vicar nor a nun. In short, while I believed I had a vocation, that God wanted me to denounce the world and devote my life to him, I had a difficult time convincing others of this. After several directionless years, I swung in and out of depression, self-harming and drinking too much. I felt angry and foolish and let down. Eventually I found my way into psychotherapy and began a long process of healing. I began to understand some things about myself, such as, how much I needed to believe I was special and chosen by God. How easy it was for someone like me to readily think of myself as an empty vessel waiting to be filled, to believe, literally that in order to glorify God I had to become as nothing. It was easier for me to believe these things, to believe in my own sinfulness, than to believe in the compassion of Christ.

For a while, I flirted with Buddhism but found that I was unable to sit still or conform to organised religion. I think I was attracted to it because I knew and admired several Buddhists and I wanted to be like them. During this time I had a significant dream –

*I am sitting in a lecture theatre listening to a talk about Buddhism, struggling to take notes. Suddenly one of the walls begins to dissolve and open out. I find that I am looking out over a green landscape, being taken on a guided tour of the sacred sites – the standing stones, fogous and white horses. I wake up knowing that everything I need, everything I have been looking for is under my feet.*

It took several years to take in the meaning of this dream, to understand where it was leading, to understand what I was supposed to *do* exactly. It was when I finally stopped trying that Druidry found me – at the point when I was finally able to listen and to honour what was arising from within me.

I attended my first ever druid camp this year. I got there because of some bones. While I am training in psychotherapy, I have a part time job in a university library. One of my responsibilities is the bones and models collection – which includes some human bone. The decision has been to deaccession these and dispose of them. In the past we have made use of a commercial company, but this time as I was phoning up for costings for yellow plastic boxes, I found I could no longer ignore the enormous guilt I was feeling. I could not think of these bones as "clinical waste". Somewhere in the recesses of my mind I remembered reading about Honouring the Ancient Dead, and after a bit of googling around found a contact number for Bobcat (the Druid name of Emma Restall Orr). This was my first contact with a druid – she was enormously helpful and encouraging, and quite practical. This encouraged me to read a bit more about druidry – and then I realised that was the nearest way to describe the path I am on. The bones of these ancestors brought me home.

I no longer need to look for teachers, or guides. These are my teachers. Stone, bone, mud, fox and owl. The fogou, the standing stone, Cornish granite and rough-hewn marble from Iona. Quartz washed up on a beach in Wales. Crow and gull and pheasant. The fat spiders who weave their webs in my garden. Hazel, Oak and Yew. Demeter and Persephone, Rhiannon and Blodeuwedd stepping out of their stories and into mine. A particularly talented group of horses in the Forest of Dean. The earth herself in all her moods whether harsh, frozen and withholding or green and fertile and dancing with life.

I never was ordained, but I create my own altars now. I think now I will go and pick marigolds and offer them to my gods, in gratitude for all that has changed and continues to change.

Sarah Kral (Creirwy). Sarah lives on the welsh borderlands. Her catholic background prompted her search for spirituality and from listening to the hills, seeing the magic of trees and her study of the Tarot she came to her pagan path in her early teens. In 2004 she joined the Order of Bards, Ovates and Druids and is currently befriending her Darkness in the Ovate grade. She doesn't like me saying this (for she's far too humble) but I call her a 'Tarot Reader Extraordinaire.'

## Sarah's Story

All my childhood was full of the stories of Jesus and God. Since I went to a Catholic school when I was younger its hardly surprising! The morning of prayers, the serenity of the adjacent convent to the school and the deep spiritual energy I picked up from the Sisters there at the school all add to my fascination and love of the stories.

It might seem disrespectful to some, but for me growing up at that time and now with the energies of the Bard within me, I can not help but just think of the New Testament as a wonderful collection of stories to inspire, strengthen and heal ourselves. Whilst I was never a 'believer' in the dogma of Catholicism or even Christianity as a whole, I feel that that doesn't stop me from loving the stories. It could just be that they remind me of a happy time at that school, or the peace that seemed to radiate from that place and the Sisters that held those energies there, in the name of love for their God. Any thing that inspired and was sacred to them is good enough for me!

I've always felt that whilst a lot of people leave Christianity and come to a more pagan or druidic way of life they often throw out the baby with the bath water. Whilst the people, the dogma and whole 'churchianity' aspect can restrict and confine our individual paths, the stories of Jesus, his parables and teachings are ones of freedom and liberation. Whether Jesus was real or not, or even if he was actual son of God or was just a wise person isn't and wasn't important to me. I don't have to believe in Buddhism to gain wisdom from the Dalai Lama neither do I need to believe in Jesus for him to touch me. As I work more with druidry and the search for wisdom that started my druidic path, I realise that its not the source of wisdom that's important, but to accept and acknowledge it wherever it is. As a druid it's important for me to read the bible and feel the messages that Jesus brought to us. Reading the stories that highlight the principles of forgiveness and being good to each other, of humanity that loves and protects, heals and restores, is something just as sacred to my druidic path as listening to the birds and meditating with a tree. Naturally my rational and over-thinking brain will come with a hundred reasons not to listen, be it the questionable source of the stories and books collected in the bible, the authors and who was the final editor of it etc. But when I read the stories now, or remember hearing them as a child, the universal truths that are there are too important to a spiritual journey to be ignored.

I've always had a belief in God/Goddess/Divinity. And I feel that will never leave me. For me that is a truth that can not be taken away, but its not that truth that underpins the goodness in the Jesus story. Like the myths of Gods and Goddess, the tales of the land and the songs in the air, whether true or not, the stories are purely inspired. They are a product of awen or divine inspiration and who am I to judge them as unimportant? As a druid I admire and respect awen because to me all beings created on this earth are parts of God. My druidic path is one seeking truth and love and for me the bible and its stories are part of God and its magic within us.

Kim Lloyd (Eala Serenarian). Kim lives in south Wales, UK, and is currently looking to get into teaching. Aside from that, she walks in the woods and writes a lot.

## Christian to Druid: A Personal Journey

Like most people of my age (I'm in my twenties) and living in a small mining town hidden among the valleys of south Wales, I was brought up as a Christian. My family is a mixed bag of Christian traditions - Catholic on one side, Protestant on the other. As a result I was raised in a Church of England household, free to go to church if I chose to, but the decision was my own. In my eighteenth summer I began to question my spirituality. I looked into other organised religions and began to read the Bible, as well as other holy books and scripture. Within them all I found the same moral codes and similar stories, their differences being the way they were presented and the individuals depicted. At that time, I became a fan of Jesus. This puzzled me at the time, as I was moving away from Christianity quite quickly with the discovery of nature-based religions, which seemed to be calling to me very loudly. But Jesus seemed to be an inspiration.

I was drawn to the qualities he seemed to exude - a wise man, a listener, and a healer. He was a man with charisma, who was honest and kind and always had time for everyone. I sought to extol these virtues in my own life and this wonderful man seemed to be a fantastic example. However, I felt strongly that my attraction to him was as a human being and not as the Son of God. As a priest he was immensely inspirational to me, even if I did not follow his teachings. I was saddened at all that the religion named after him has become, and the hate and intolerance that some modern fundamentalists spread through the world. I knew this was not his fault, and that if he were alive today he would most likely be trying to repair the damage.

I also began to see parallels between the Christ myth and the Pagan mythologies that I was learning about. I saw a similarity in the tales of Christ's birth and the birth of the Mabon, at the same time of the year. I began to feel that instead of a godhead, Jesus to me represented an archetype. With this freedom of knowledge, I began to look at Celtic Christianity. I am fiercely proud of my Welsh heritage and my Celtic roots and this seemed a logical progression. From that, I moved on to Druidry. Druidry was the proverbial kick up the backside that I needed. I had been seeking a tradition that was well-rounded. One that had its home here in Britain, and was not of foreign lands. One that was academic and yet experiential. A tradition that was equally open to community and solitary practice. One that could be wild and also civilised. I found all those in Druidry. I had a powerful dream one night that changed my thinking. In it, beside my bed there sat a wooden box made of oak. Inside was a rosary made of seeds. One by one, the rosary burst into life and produced many oak saplings. I glimpsed the most powerful message yet from my guides that Druidry was my calling. Now and again, when I pray to Cernunnos and to Rhiannon,[73] every few months or so, I spot Jesus standing against a tree, watching and smiling.

Pauline Kennedy Allan (Potia). Pauline lives and works in Glasgow. She works as a University administrator. She is married and blessed with two children. She is a member of the Pagan Federation Scotland, the Druid Network and the Association of Polytheist Traditions. She is also involved in the local interfaith community.

## Dancing with Jesus

Like many Pagans I come from a background of Christianity, to be precise high Church of England. As a child I went to Sunday school in different places as my family moved around. For a while I went to a Catholic convent boarding school in Sussex and this place was a much loved home for my time there. After that I went to a convent day school in London and had the distinction of being the only non-catholic pupil there at that time. While living in London my family went to a local Church of England where I became a server. I also sang in the church choir. By my own choice there was a time when I went to church twice on most Sundays, once serving at the early morning service and again singing in the choir for the later family service. When I was about 16 I chose to get confirmed and at the time I sincerely believed every word I said during that confirmation rite.

After that however I began to question things more and more. I began to notice that many in the church community were very good at saying the right words but very poor at doing the right things. They didn't seem to "walk their talk". This was brought home to me in a couple of incidents in particular, one involving a member of my family who was extremely ill. She was on the church prayer list but hardly anyone asked how she was and noone ever asked if we needed practical help or support in any way. In fact the only offer of practical help we received was from some Jehovah's Witnesses who used to call every now and then with their magazine the Watchtower. None of us were members of their community but they were the only ones that asked if we needed any practical help and I have never forgotten that. There were other events that I won't go into here but needless to say I became more and more disillusioned with the church community and as a result with Christianity.

When I left home to go to University I tried again with the student branch of the Scripture Union but again I found people who seemed more interested in their talk than really trying to live their path. I stopped associating with any of them after one of them criticised me for giving a friend a fried egg sandwich when he was hungry because he'd spent his student grant already and couldn't afford any food. I was told I was only encouraging him in careless spending habits.

For the next few years I read around a number of different spiritual paths including some esoteric and new age materials. I referred to myself as pagan friendly if anyone asked but at that time I didn't consider myself to be a pagan. Later in 1997 I started walking a pagan path and found a home in Druidry. Here I found people who were generally keen on "walking their talk" and who encouraged me to take personal responsibility for my own spiritual development and my own actions.

My path in the forest of Druidry has been at times a complicated one and at other times a very simple one. I have been blessed along the way with some wonderful friends and I have met some very inspiring individuals. Oddly enough it is as a Pagan that I have also met some of the most lovely and genuine Christians, people who are deeply connected to their own path and not at all judgmental of others.

A few months ago I was inspired to look at my own underlying principles and values, at what qualities were the most important to me. After much thought I came up with three main principles or virtues, Love, Truth and Duty (the ones you choose and not the ones others try and inflict upon you). The most important of these to me is Love and the best way I have of defining this principle in a few words is "Love thy neighbour as thyself". Not often easy to do but worth striving for in my opinion. I realised that while my outward methods had changed the principles that guided me along my path were the same as when I was a child.

More recently still, following on from conversations in online forums I was inspired to consider my confirmation vows. Keeping my word is very important to me and again it has been for as long as I can remember so what did that mean in relation to my confirmation. I came to the conclusion after a lot of thought and some discussion with other friends that while I had been sincere I did not at that time have the full picture to really understand the implications of what I was saying. I also realised that it wasn't the childhood spiritual friend of Jesus that I was rejecting but the earthbound organisation of the church.

As a polytheist pagan I have developed relationships with a few deities and while I have not included the deity I knew as "JC" in my thoughts for a long time I could not reject the comfort I found in that relationship as a child. So I found myself doing the spiritual equivalent of phoning that long lost friend and making contact again. I don't know where this will lead, I have grown and changed as all children do. I have other gods that I talk to now but although I have grown away from my childhood understanding of Jesus I can still respect and honour the lessons I learnt and the relationship I had with him. And just maybe I'll forge a new relationship with the essence of a being for whom Love was and is an essential part.

# Chapter 19

# The American Indians and the Celts

*This we know. The earth does not belong to man. Man belongs to the earth. This we know. All things are connected like the blood which unites one family. All things are connected. Whatever befalls the earth, befalls the sons of the earth. Man did not weave the web of life; he is merely a strand in it. Whatever he does to the web, he does to himself.*
Chief Seattle (c. 1786 - 1866)

Lisabeth Ryder has a doctorate from University of California in Linguistic Anthropology and has done field work in several Native American communities and in Papua New Guinea, where she lived for four years. She is a life-long activist and currently is working in labour organizing.

## Terrible Beauty

Since childhood, I have had misgivings about certain implications of Christian faith, and primary among these is the meaning and historicity of salvation. Two thousand years ago the world population was some 300 million people. How could a just and loving God condemn generations of children to eternal damnation who lived, say, before the time of Christ or in the Americas prior to the Age of Discovery?

Even to a child's mind, in the retelling of a story misinterpretations creep in. Like a game of "Telephone" - the child's game where the first child in a circle whispers something in the ear of the next child, who whispers in the ear of the next, and so around the circle, until the last child says out loud what he heard - which is completely different from what the first child said. Somewhere along the line they must have gotten it wrong. Questions like these have guided me away from formulaic Christianity where the only concern is that you regularly check off a laundry list of beliefs to assure your own safe conduct through the Gates of Heaven. I have instead pursued the mystic's path. With absolute faith in God's love I have embarked on a quest into how God has revealed Himself to other cultures. Not to convert or embrace a different faith, but to open myself up to the broader language of God. I became an Anthropologist and studied the cultures and languages of the world.

After earning my doctorate from the University of California, I turned my attention to the mythology and lore of my own heritage. As a child, my grandmother told me that her people came over from Ireland on the back of a great white horse. So I knew I was of Irish heritage; but there was just a little problem with geography.

That horse took me for a wild ride until I met Manannan mac Lir, the sea god of the Tuatha Dé Danann and the magical horses of the Sidhe (shee), the ancient fairy folk of Ireland. "When the tempest breaks over the sea in Ireland, the breakers are said to be the white horses of Manannan mac Lir."[74]

Along that road, I also met the Celtic Druids who were employed in all the pursuits I loved. The Druids were story-tellers, poets, historians, jurists, healers, scholars, political advisors and spiritual leaders. They were the learned elite of Celtic society, leaders of a nature-based spirituality when the sacred and secular worlds were not alienated.

For the Druids all of nature was imbued with the spirit of God, for example, each tree had a spirit. Their place of worship was among the oak groves in the richly adorned beauty of God's creation, rather than locked in a man-made edifice cluttered with human-defined wealth. Certainly Christ's focus was not on surrounding himself with wealth — Luke 12:27: "Consider the lilies, how they grow: they neither toil nor spin; and yet I say to you, even Solomon in all his glory was not arrayed like one of these."

The Druids understood the immortality of the soul, using techniques we call "magic" to bridge the otherworld and create a personal relationship with the Divine. They were mystics, who like the Magi, read the signs and interpreted God's language in the pursuit of the One Truth, what Christ called the Kingdom of God, the nature of our relationship with the Creator. While riding my magical white horse back across the misty seas to Ireland from the Land of Youth, Ti r na nOg, I like Oisin before me found three hundred years had elapsed in my absence. My family had emigrated from Ireland in the 1700's and yet preserved in my family culture was Irish myth and legend, and a tradition of storytelling. My grandmother had been born in 1889 and was raised by people who were alive during the Civil War. Her grandfather, who had schooled her in these myths, was born just after 1800. And my grandmother's grandfather had been schooled by his grandfather who had been born in Ireland. After arriving in the Carolinas in the 1700's, my family moved to what is today Sumpter county Alabama. At that time, it was part of the Choctaw nation. They were living there in 1834 when they lost their young daughter, Martha, who is buried there. After the Civil War, they moved to Arkansas where they bought the land my mother and grandmother were born on with a Choctaw land scrip. Many Irish families lived among the Choctaw, and with good reason. The Choctaw had myths and legends similar to the Irish. They had stories of "Little People" who lived in the forest known as Kowi Anukasha (meaning "Forest Dwellers"). Bohpoli, elf-like forest folk, would capture young children playing in the forest and take them back to a cave. There, three items would be offered to the child: a knife, poisonous herbs, and medicinal herbs. If the child chose the medicinal herbs, he would grow up to be a healer and Bohpoli would assist him in learning his art and in producing medicines. Like the Ban Sidhe (banshee), the screech of the Ishkitini portended death. Numerous other "Little People" occupied Choctaw myth, ranging from playful sprites, to shape shifters, or odious and malign spirits that could capture a person's spirit.

The Choctaw lived in the Southeast United States, in what is today Mississippi and Alabama, some of the most fertile land along the Mississippi River. Like the Irish, they were spiritual, rather than economic, farmers with a sacred relationship with the land. They were the premier agriculturalists of the Southeast, every year producing a surplus, and supplying their neighbors. They lived in villages and farmed corn, beans, and squash in the rich Mississippi flood plain, and developed a democratic form of governance with elected leaders. The wealth and stability created by their industry led to a richly cultured life engaging in sports — a stick ball game akin to lacrosse (a game played with two sticks but otherwise resembling Irish game hurling). A complex spiritual life was focused around sacred mounds (like the fairy mounds of Ireland), mythologically connected to their origins and the source of domesticated corn.

Because the Choctaw were the strong and established economic centerpiece of the Native American Southeast, the US government targeted them to be the first of the tribes removed to Oklahoma. Ironically, the Choctaw had fought at the side of Andrew Jackson at what has been touted as the most important battle fought on American soil, the Battle of New Orleans, where British forces were decisively and finally repelled in 1814. Yet, in 1834 Andrew Jackson authored and executed the plan to dispossess the Choctaw of their land creating a man-made famine, claiming the lives of a third of the Choctaw population. The Choctaw was the initial tribe removed from their land in the Trail of Tears so that their land could be converted into planta-tions by wealthy slave owners.

Sixteen years later, to foreclose on properties, the British overlords in Ireland seized upon the opportunity created by the potato blight [the phytophthora infestans fungus] which destroyed the crop sustaining the poor tenant farmers of Ireland. There was enough food in Ireland to feed everyone, yet the British shipped the grain crops and sheep overseas to be sold for profit, while they expanded their land holdings by evictions, using starvation and migration to rid Ireland of "surplus" Irish.

The stories of the Choctaw and the Irish are dramas repeated throughout the nineteenth and twentieth centuries, genocide motivated by greed and precipitated by racism. In the period between 1830 and 1850 the Native American and Irish societies were despoiled by man-made famines in a land-grab consolidating the South into a slave-plantation economy and solidifying the English aristocracy's enclosures of Irish land. In 1848, the Choctaw took up a collection and sent it to the Irish famine victims. Even though their society had been devastated by the avarice of the new immigrants, they saw the commonality of their struggles. The Choctaw gift, a few hundred dollars painstakingly collected among the destitute, is a legacy - a statement against greed, against racism, against the terrible policies of displacement and extermination haunting our recent history.

What this story tells us about the world we could live in makes it timeless. To be able to see the commonality in these tragedies, instead of being consumed by misery and loss, is the vision of "terrible beauty". The Choctaw gift is a moment of powerful human spirit bringing to mind the words of William Butler Yeats, "All changed, changed utterly: A terrible beauty is born." The Choctaw showed us the path - the simple act of seeing our common humanity and acting upon it in any way we can.

This compassion says to me that God has revealed Himself to the Choctaw. God is inclusive and breathes grace into all human hearts, not just Christians. Surely the Choctaw were more "Christian" than the Christians who stole their land and attempted to exterminate them. Jesus did not ask us to wear a badge saying; "I am a Christian" to distinguish us from all else. He asked us to simply love thy neighbor as thyself. My spiritual journey has not led me to any single denomination, or even religion, because to choose one credo over another only creates divisions. Instead I seek a direct relationship with God and experience God by nurturing compassion. God reveals himself in all of the spiritual paths. God is Love. Compassion means many things, for example, forgiving those who would do us harm —- 'turning the other cheek' —- or giving to the poor, but it means more than that. Rather than an intellectual or emotional ascent to abstracts, compassion has to be actualized. It is not enough to say "I love" and feel warm all over, one must live spiritually. We need to act on love as the Choctaw.

Jesus was born into a society governed by strict "cleanliness" laws. Someone who did not have the wealth to adhere to the strict dietary rules or was disadvantaged, for example, blind, disabled, or diseased was excluded from the temple as unclean. Prostitutes were also unclean and this status was inherited. Jesus' ministry broke down the stranglehold the wealthy had on the temples and once again allow everyone to approach God directly.

Jesus healed the sick and ministered to the poor, but he also worked to right the injustices of the system. First he threw the money-changers out of the temple. Then he threw out the complex religious laws, replacing them with only two commandments: love God with all thy heart and love thy neighbor as thyself. And finally he moved worship out of the temple, to the mount, where everyone could have access to the Kingdom of God. For breaking down this system of injustice, the elders of the temple turned him over to the Romans to crucify.

If we know that society has injustices but we are faring adequately, even within those structures of injustice, giving to a charity or volunteering at a soup kitchen costs little and allows the system to remain in place. The greater act of compassion is to work for social justice. Like Jesus, the Dalai Lama and the Druids, we need to take an active role in changing policy, rectifying injustices and guiding society's progress.

In my search for true compassion, I work, both globally and locally, on human rights, labor and environmental issues, such as global warming, to help save our planet, God's creation, along with the beings that live here. I hear the echoes of Jesus' ministry when the Dalai Lama implores, living compassion for all sentient beings is our own salvation.

*(To follow on from Liz's powerful and moving piece the next story has been written by a member of the Choctaw Tribe)*

Gary Whitedeer is an artist, writer, and son of a tribal elder of the Choctaw tribe. He is an amazing man who puts his spirituality into practice in many ways, not least his bridge-building work between his own people and the Celtic culture of Ireland. The following piece clearly ties in with what you will have read in the previous essay by Liz Rider.

## A Spiritual Practicality

In the Choctaw worldview, all of nature is animated by *aiyokchaya*, or life force, a spiraling flow of endless combinations of spirit strands from which species emerge. Within a universe that is both substance and spirit, seen and unseen, everything is alive, connected like beads on a cosmic necklace by threads of life force. A creator known as *Hushi Atahali* has the responsibility for crafting the unfolding design of the cosmic necklace, the ordering of the natural world.

Despite its anomalies this ordering is considered perfect in intent, and as a people the Choctaw have altered it very little. Like beads on a necklace, the Choctaw seek harmony within the grand design rather than contriving change, and throughout time have chosen to coexist with the natural world. Time is the current that makes life force flow, and time is viewed as cyclical. The forward motion of time regulates a continuous, circular movement between the seen and unseen. Substance flows clockwise into spirit, and spirit flows clockwise into substance, birth into death, death to birth.

Anomalies in the grand design which include human failings corrupt the life current, resulting in imbalance, disorder, disharmony, and finally, unhappiness. Because corruption is inherent in the grand design, it is managed and mitigated by either achieving or restoring balance, a perpetual first condition that may be very generally defined as moderation. Balance in turn begets order, or propriety. Balance and order beget harmony, a way of standing in good relation to the universe.

Balance, order, and harmony finally beget happiness, or human contentment on the circular flow of time. These primary premises are the foundations of tribal life, and may be called the Choctaw Way. Formal culture and social lifeways ensue from a secondary or appendage belief system realized through a people having a down-to-earth practicality imbued with an abiding sense of the mystic. Inevitably, there has always been a practical peering ahead along the time spiral.

One tribal prophecy predicts that invaders from either Asia or the Middle East will someday occupy America. The Choctaw will be spared if they hang their traditional shirts in front of their houses as identifying markers. Tribal oral history also runs deep. An origin account remembers that an ancient priesthood class directed the work of raising *Nanih Waiya*, an earthen platform temple mound. The earthwork still stands, dating to about the time of Christ.

Choctaw society evolved as a temple mound culture, with *Nanih Waiya* the centerpiece of a national capitol encircled by a city wall two miles in circumference. For millennia, the Choctaw observed the totality of the world around them and found life to be good. While the tribal view then purports that humans are also essentially good but susceptible to corruption, the missionaries of the 1800s espoused that humans are essentially base, but susceptible to salvation.

Certainly the Choctaw needed salvation from colonialism, and when missionary notions of an all-saving grace were wedded to an organized insistence that the Choctaw Way was evil and pagan, an enduringly toxic mix of hope and shame permeated the tribal psyche. After American treaties dwindled the national estate, ethnic cleansings began in earnest, prodded by bayonet. Those Choctaw who managed to avoid the brutal death marches became isolated and impoverished; strangers in their own land.

The missionary's messiah exhorted the Choctaw to prevail

upon the slender mercies of their oppressors, who demanded their homelands and traditions in exchange for second-class status and second-hand religion. Even as lands were lost many traditions survived, and curative practitioners, heirs to the old temple mound priesthoods, continue today. *Alikchi* or Choctaw doctors are still essential to those traditional communities where significant portions of the original worldview are maintained.

Whenever corruption cannot be managed, *alikchi* intercede to restore balance. *Alikchi* are born to their callings, allowed to apprentice only if they have an innate gift to diagnose and heal. There are four classes of contemporary Choctaw doctors, a balance of sorts. *Hopaiyee* were originally war prophets and now act as seers. *Alikchi* proper are healers. *Isht a Hullo* are healers also, but prone to malice. *Hothkunna* are those who have corrupted their healing gifts in order to practice malice entirely.

Besides performing diagnoses, *alikchi* remove ailments from patients by horn suction and have used plant life to successfully treat diseases ranging from congestive heart failure, to cancer, to diabetes. Protections are prepared for homes, properties, and individuals. *Alikchi* also mitigate against *afitobah*; paranormal harm. As varied as their abilities are, the Choctaw doctors have no real remedies for one particularly implacable corruption. It is spirit blindness, attrition of the mystic.

American colonialism and its economic models have prompted an accelerating consumerism, with business managers supplanting traditional leaders. Choctaw churches still run by mission boards have replaced tribal ceremonies. Generations of relentless intermarriage within the American mainstream has bred a burgeoning white diaspora that proclaims distant tribal ties. Not surprisingly, there has been a proportionate erosion of spiritual sensibilities and a parallel abandonment of the Choctaw Way.

Yet a few core communities still see the world through Choctaw eyes, valuing consensus over raw ambition, quiet strength above self-promotion and cooperation more than competition. In these communities balance is still sought within the grand design. Accordingly, a symbiotic equilibrium has been achieved through Choctaw *dualism*, a spiritual practicality that allows for coexistence with Christianity, colonialism, and consumerism at acceptable nexuses of shifting substance and an older, abiding sense of the mystic.

Dualism quietly harmonizes the Choctaw Way with Christian professions of love and harmony, tenets which appeal to tribal values. In core communities, many Choctaw churchgoers rely on their own curative practitioners to help restore balance. As a viable counterpoise, the intercessions of *alikchi* are not considered as either evil or pagan. Dualism validates the Choctaw Way, with Christian tenets employed as a natural complement to the older order despite sporadic censure from the pulpit.

Western-style education, the English language, and American political and economic models are potent agents of colonialism. Against a tireless onslaught of acculturation spanning two centuries, traditional Choctaws have found another quiet balance. A college education and what might be considered a good job are viewed as corrupting only if they take members out of the community, effectively ending their roles as communal relatives, community contributors, and full-time tribal members.

Consumerism is a strong challenge to the original worldview because much of its attraction is rooted in an intergenerational sense of poverty, of being denied the American dream. With disposable incomes increasing, many Choctaws now roam stores and shopping malls on gratuitous sprees. Also at play may be imbedded traces of a once highly successful indigenous economy that sustained a lively quality of life for a very long time without the distraction of daily struggle.

Seeds of consumerism seem to be visceral. The Choctaw once depleted their deer population for the rifles and goods of French traders, causing wars with distant tribes over hunting grounds. Such historic imbalance is hard to reconcile with the Choctaw Way. My father, a Choctaw elder, has a mildly impressive bank account but lives very simply. He once posed the question, "How much is enough?" a consideration for Choctaw dualism that has much wider resonance.

For the moment and for millennia the Choctaw way of seeing exists. Dualism, while somewhat denaturing as long-term compromise, has nevertheless made it possible for traditional communities to remain recognizable and consistent in language and by worldview to other tribal cycles, other eras. Worldview is realized through community, and traditional tribal settlements actively sustain the Choctaw Way; which would otherwise devolve into mere philosophy.

In comparing the Choctaw Way it should be noted that although the tribal worldview has eroded, its remaining essentials have continued uninterrupted. While the existing Choctaw belief system may have key patterns in common with say, ancient Druidism, revitalizations of such latent philosophies are inevitably informed by subsequent cultural filters, and often lack community ethos through which to realize and maintain core ideas. Conversely, loss of ethos would not necessarily invalidate attempts to regenerate dormant worldviews, efforts which may succeed on other levels.

Somewhere back along the great curve of time the Choctaws are singing, and our songs now are echoes of those living distant sounds. Everything is alive. There is a flow to the universe. As we continue to seek balance we know that life is intended to be good. We are all as beads in a wonderful design.

This is Álvaro Herrera's second contribution. I am so grateful to him. It is a re-working of an article he submitted to the OBOD forum's 'monthly seminar'. After my wife and I spent our honeymoon in Mexico, I have been fascinated by Maya and Aztec cultures. Again, much of their spirituality seems to tie in with our own pre-Christian Celtic tradition. As a Mexican, Álvaro is well placed to write on this culture and, as a Celtic Pagan, he is also well able to show us some of the links between the two traditions.

## The Central / South American Native Tradition

There were a lot of different tribes living in what is now called America, some very different, some alike. We can't speak of a Native American lore as a whole, since it differs from the natives of what is now Canada, to the ones of what is now Chile. America is a big continent and there were a huge number of different tribes.

However one of the most emblematic civilizations were the Aztecs, the most successful of the Nahuatl tribes who inhabited the central part of Mexico, and on whose honour the country was named [the capital of their empire was called Mexico-Tenochtitlan]. I'm going to address to that specific culture in this short essay.

Since the Nahuas did not write text books, and most of their lore was orally taught in the Calmecatl or Tepochcalli (a kind of University), and just a few of their mythologies were put in the painted codes on their temples (the pyramids and so on), what has come to us is largely the work of the visiting Christian monks. As with the Irish lore, it was a great advantage to preserve the lore that otherwise would be lost in the oceans of time. However the disadvantage was the clear censorship and bias of the missionaries themselves. These texts, along with the artistic and architectural remains of their culture, have made it possible to reconstruct their philosophical thinking.

## The Universe and the Nahuatl cosmology

First we have to understand the basic cosmology of the Nahuas, regarding space and time. In his book, *La pensée cosmologique des anciens mexicains,* Jacques Soustelle states that for the Nahuas there was no beginning or ending. This concept of space-time as a whole was alien to the Western world until Einstein. However it was a day to day experience for the Nahuas. There was a particular time and place for each of the four cardinal points and the centre. Each person had a special destiny according to when and where they were born. Each one was associated with a place, time, colour, certain virtues and powers. Each person had a place and time to die. They also had a 'way' to die.

Also this continuity of events (of opposites that merge into a new one) and this model of the universe was reflected in existence. That death defines life, and life defines death is not an absolute opposition as it is for a modern western point of view. It is not seen as the natural end of life, it is only one phase of an infinite cycle. Life and Death are interlinked; they flow together for eternity as complementary ways. Life had no higher function than to flow into death. Death was not an end in itself; it was only a way to re-establish the universal balance, to re-establish the debts that the humans had with their gods, and to ensure the continuity of society and the cosmos itself.

## The Society, the Self and the Nahuas

The second important thing to take into account was the concept of individuals and society.

For the Aztecs, the individual plays just a role in the web of life; it is part of this immense cosmos, interlinked with each and every creature, mountain, river, etc. Sacrifice was not a form of individual salvation for the other world, but cosmic health. The individual sacrifice's itself for his tribe, but also for his world. The need of human blood was not to feed the hunger of the gods in a literal way; it was a way of bringing equilibrium and salvation to the cosmos. The Universe's equilibrium was more important than even a person's life.

Western civilization views this as a cult of death - a savage and cruel religious path. But that is just a lack of understanding of the meaning of death. Death was not worshiped as an entity, nor worshiped as an end in itself. It was part of the continuum, a phase to go through. Warriors sacrificed themselves to the gods. There were ball games (very similar to today's football but played with the hip instead of the foot) to symbolize the movement of the cosmos, and the winning team - the one who established how the cosmos will be moving - gave their lives as a reward, as a form of ensuring that their way will be preserved.

I'm not going to attempt to analyze the Western (Christian and Greco-Latin) point of view, since they are well known worldwide, and I take for granted that the reader has studied this at school, and could see it reflected in their civilization, whether you are Christian or not. The influence of this cosmology has given form to the cosmology of today's western world. So I leave it to the reader to make the comparisons.

## The Division of the Universe

Nahuatl people divided the Universe into Three - The Upperworld, made up of thirteen skies, The Middle world, made up of three realms, and the Underworld, which is in the form of a pyramid with nine levels.

*The thirteen skies*
These were the 13 skies for the Nahuas:
the sky of the stars given by Tonacatecuhtli, two stars, one male, one female, that will take care of humankind forever.
the sky of the 400 (meaning infinite) stars, Citlalco
the sky of the sun, Ilhuicatl Tonatiuh
the sky of Venus, called in Nahuatl Citlalpol or big star
the sky of the comets, of flaming stars, Citlain popoca

the sky of day

the sky of night, these two were associated with of green and blue, or black and blue

the sky of tempest

The sky of white

The sky of yellow

The sky of red; on these three skies (8, 9 & 10) were where the gods lived, the Teteocan

The skies of Omeyocan, where the source of generation and life Ometeotl, the dual god who was at the same time male and female, or a mixed neutral being who create everything that existed.

## The Middle world

There were three realms in the middle or horizontal world, the land called Anahuatl or Cem-anahuatl (meaning the ring surrounded by water), the oceans called teoatl (teo meaning divine or godly and atl meaning water) and the heavens known as ilhuica atl (the water of the sky, since it merges with the water that the men could touch).

## The Underworld

Finally we arrived to the underworld, the Way to the Mictlan.

For the Nahuas, there where three ways to die:

The first was to die in battle. The warriors who were brave but could not defeat their enemies, went to the third sky - the one of the sun, Ilhuicatl Tonatiuh. There they were merged with the sun god Tonatiuh as companions for all eternity. It was the most prestigious way of departing this world.

To this sky also joined the pregnant women who die in childbirth, since childbirth was viewed as a battle between the mother and the child. They were known as cihuateteo, and they were the ones who return to the earth to take the souls of the warriors who die in battle. Also the babies who die in childbirth were sent to the 12 & 13 skies - back to the source, back to Ometeotl.

The second way of dying was death caused by water, including being killed by lighting. The ones who died like this were sent to the Tlaloctlan, described as the eternal summer place, were Tlaloc (the god of water) lived. This otherworld was full of wisdom and joy, and the ones who died in this way were meant to be the Tlaloques or Tlaloc assistants.

For the people who died of any other cause was the Mictlan. To get to the Mictlan, the dead people were supposed to pass through nine levels that prove they were worthy to reside forever in the Yolomictlantzinco or the Heart of the Mictlan. First they needed to cross the Chignahuapan, a great river, where they meet Xolotl, a god in the form of a Xoloitzcuintle, a hairless dog originally from Mexico who would guide them and help them to cross to the other side of the river. They were advised to not to follow the dog with white hair, nor the one with black hair, even when they offer them any treat, for they would never lead them to the other side.

Once they crossed, they would pass the path of the two mountains that demolish everything. There they were inflicted with great and several injuries. They would loose their clothes and their bodies would start to break up. Then they would have to cross the obsidian mountain, were their bodies would be cut down and start to bleed.

After this they would cross a valley where, the freezing north wind (which cuts everything like obsidian knifes) would attack them. Here their bodies would be cut until only the heart and bones survive.

On the fifth level, they would have to deliver all their flags, to the ones who keep them. After that they would arrive to the valley where the arrows are thrown.

The seventh level, was seen as the place where the beasts would eat their hearts. They were supposed to fight them to save their hearts, the only part of them that they still have.

The eighth level was the place of the dark water, or the dark mist, were they would have to find (by themselves) the way out in almost complete darkness

Finally they would arrive at the heart of the Mictlan - the ninth level - where Mictlantecutli and Mictecacihuatl, the Lord and Lady of the Dead, lived. They were portrayed as human skeletons with little or no flesh, and dark hair where the 400 stars reflected. They would welcome them and assure them a place in that level, and there they could live without worry, with pulque (an alcoholic drink) and food given to them. There, at last, they could party and have fun. They would be light beings, with only their skeleton and heart, united by their light energy.

## This lore and the present

One of the biggest contributions this lore can make to our present day is their approach to death - their spiritual and intellectual approach. Death is just a phase, a journey to other worlds. Either you believe that the soul returns to life (reincarnation) or that it is born to new life in the otherworld, where it will live forever. If you deny death, you'll be denying life. Embrace it, play with it, joke with it and respect it. Acknowledge that you are part of a web of life, that every life is sacred, that no killing is justified if it's not for your own survival. See that the every being that dies is not a mere statistic, nor a collateral damage; all are part of our cosmos,

All this philosophy is currently reflected in the mixed culture that is Mexico, a country that has make a syncretism of the native cultures and the European one. One of the best books ever written about this is The Labyrinth of Solitude by the literature novel price, the Mexican Octavio Paz, who explains better than anyone who I ever read, this mixture.

Many have said that the old inhabitants of what is now Mexico were a culture of death. It's a common misunderstanding.

Death was about the regeneration of cosmos itself, sacrifice and transcendence, and a view of death that face it fearlessly and with respect.

Death has lost its place in modern culture. It is not mentioned in casual talks, nor is it taken into account within other spheres of live. It is suppressed everywhere - in political pronouncements, commercial advertising, public morality and popular customs. The western culture is a culture of life, or so they say. However death is still around but, to the popular view, it's just something that happens and is therefore ignored.

So, death is feared on a personal level, but taken without any meaning in a social one. That is one of the big differences that these cosmologies have. Quoting Mr. Paz:

And Remember: Death is the mirror of life; life is the mirror of death.

## How this Lore is applicable to Druidry

We can apply this in several ways, from comparative religion, to the use of the rituals, myths and legends, to our inner exploration.

First at all I recommend that, before applying this, you read more about the Mexican myths, lore and traditions. Get immersed in this world. The approach into a new pantheon has to be done with a lot of work and taken seriously. One of the biggest complaints of the Native American people, when westerners 'borrow' precious insights, tools and spiritual lessons from their culture, is the lack of respect in gaining appropriate knowledge of the cultural background. So, before trying a "shamanic" journey to the Mictlan, or creating an Aztec themed ancestor altar for Samhain, or an exploration of an inner voyage, I strongly suggest you get more information about where are you going to go, and whom you may encounter.

As for me this is what I have tried when approaching the

Celtic deities, to be immersed in their culture and traditions, to know their story and history; to be respectful and take things step by step. As you may have seen, there are a lot of commonalities between the two cosmologies, which make it easier to move between them. For me it is an approach to my two root beliefs; one which links to my European ancestors, and one that comes from my cultural indigenous ancestors. That does not mean that a person without a native American ancestry can't approach this way, but he or she must be prepared to put in a lot of hard work and respect.

# Conclusion

There is, of course, no possible way I can write a satisfactory conclusion to this book.

'Why,' you may ask?

Because, though I have told the story of my own dis and re-enchantment, and though I have allowed others to share theirs, none of them are finished, none have been concluded, and neither is yours. That's why it's all such a great adventure, a Grail Quest no less.

So while writing this book has been an incredible journey, what strikes me is that the real voyage has actually only just begun. There is so much more. The world is an enchanted place and I look forward to uncovering more magic as I tread this new and exciting path.

The Christ still accompanies me, but I now see him as the divine spark in all humanity – and all religions. He is the light known by many names – the radiant sun that brightens our path and illuminates our way.

In many forms he comes to wake us from our sleep – to bring us back to life. This is the power of the ancient sun-god myths that preceded even the Nazarene. My own attempt at such a myth is this poem, which I use when, by 'magic', I make a golden sun appear from an empty dark cloth:

Yule
*The Earth Mother sleeps*
*A sleeping beauty fair,*
*Who while in slumber, all around her, dark and cold and bare.*

*She waits for the kiss.*
*On which she survives*
*Her heart yearns, the wheel turns, the prince of light arrives*

*He parts the darkened blankets*
*Leans forth with lips of gold*
*The earth quakes, the princess wakes, the solstice lord – behold!*

*Whenever there is darkness*
*And love gives way to fear*
*Think on this, the sun-god's kiss, and the light will re-appear.*

The adventure has not been comfortable, mainly because of the pressures caused by my own decision to take the action I took back in May 2007. I do not know what further developments will occur. I sometimes wonder whether, by the time this book is published, I will still be living where I do, and with whom I do. My deepest longing – my dream – is that all wounds can be healed and that the pressures caused are relieved, to the point where my beautiful wife and I are at last free to begin enjoying what we have (the magic that is under our feet but which neither of us has been able to fully see). Only time will tell.

Whatever, I still hold that I was right to make that move. Honesty is always the better way. Reputation, praise, reward and respect all mean absolutely nothing if they are based on an inauthentic life. There are many such lives lived out within the world of the institutional Church – *it breeds them like rabbits*. I am no longer prepared to live in such a world. Truth and honesty may well often cause much pain, but at least the pain can then begin to be healed, because what caused the pain in the first place is now open like a cut left un-bandaged to breathe.

Yet after everything I've said, and after everything I've been through, I still love the dear old C of E... so tenderly. She had been my mother for two decades, and even unwanted children still feel connected to their parents. So, though radical and unconventional I remain an ordained member of her. This may be an embarrassment to some, but to others I know my story, and my magic, make sense. I still meet many 'Anglican Angels' out there on my travels, and they give me real hope - hope that a core of spiritual, authentic and open-minded energy stills pulses away, like a heart beat, just a little under the surface. Right now I don't know what the future holds. Will I remain somewhere between the two worlds of Christianity and Druidry forever? Will I gradually be absorbed back into the life of the former, but with a much wider vision? Or will I eventually cut my ties and become a full blown Druid? Right now I don't know and I don't care. My only concern is to remain authentic and follow the way that the wind blows. I hate labels anyway. They only serve to ensnare us inside boxes of opinion. So, Great Spirit, God/Dess of many names, breathe upon this battered soul and send him on his way, free from any constraints, open to whatever comes.

As for the Blue Raven. Oh she flies on ahead, glancing back, beckoning me on, giving me hope and ever reminding me that I too can fly.

# Epilogue – The Flight of the Blue Raven

While browsing on the internet I came across a wonderful American musician who is deeply inspired by the traditions of Native America. His name is Jeff Ball.

One piece of his really spoke to me. Not only is it hauntingly beautiful, but he preludes the song by telling a tale based on an old Native American raven myth. The song is called Flight of the Blue Raven. I'll let Jeff himself explain his inspiration:

*'I named the song Flight of the Blue Raven because the afterlife is commonly called the Blue Road in many native tribes. That, combined with the Raven's use as a symbol, or messenger of, death seemed a logical fit to me. As the song took shape it was easy to imagine the moon's light on raven's iridescent wings. In my minds eye I never clearly see the Raven... only glimpses as he flew within the barren trees. He is on a mission to deliver someone to the other side. I know it's kind of creepy but that's what I see when I hear the song.'*

This is the Tale that Jeff tells. As he explained, it is not his story. It belongs to the oral traditions of the many Native Tribes.

## Raven and the Sun

Native America is rich with legends about how things came to be. One such legend tells us how Raven brought light back to the people. It seems that long ago for reasons unknown, a great sky chief reached from his world into our own taking our sun and leaving us wrapped in darkness. But what that chief didn't know, and many people still today, is that raven's a bit of trickster. He took it upon himself to bring the light back. He flew all around the edge of our sky looking for some kind of a passage way from our world to the other... a window, a doorway or a tear that would allow him to cross. Once he found what he was looking for he made his way into the other side and down by the river's edge where he landed. He turned into a cedar seed and dropped to the bottom of the water. He stayed there through the night waiting - waiting for when that sky chief's daughter would wake and come down the next morning. And as the sun rose she did just that. She gathered that water up in her hands and brought it up to her lips and drank and as she did she took raven as that cedar seed down inside of her where he would grow for nine months... becoming the grandson of that sky chief. Years came and went and raven grew to be a small boy and he would often ask about the box up on the shelf that held the bright yellow ball. But over and again grandfather wouldn't let him play with it. But one day, as children do, he wore grandfather down. Grandfather turned and reached up onto that shelf bringing the box down, and as he turned and handed it to raven, raven took it within his hands and (right before grandfather) turned back into his bird self. As he made his way through the sky back to our world, flying hard, he got to that window bringing our light back but not without first being charred by the heat of the sun and from that day forward raven was forever the colour of night.

# Post Script

## A Collage of Enchantment

Throughout the winter of 2008, I toured various theatres with my show 'One Enchanted Evening.' My dream was to re-awaken wonder within the audience members, giving them a deep and lasting taste of real magic.

Aware that many 'Official Show Programmes' are full of adverts, and not a lot of substance, I wanted to create a Programme that contained an 'extra special something.' With the help of some wonderful friends I think I achieved my goal.

Over the years many writers, teachers, priests, druids and magicians from various walks of life, have touched me deeply with their friendship, creativity and wisdom. My idea was to contact as many of them as possible, with an invitation to contribute a sentence or two towards a unique *Collage of Enchantment.*

Because so many purchasers of the Programme appreciated this Verbal Collage I have selected some to close this book with. I trust that you, too, will find the following words to be a rich source of inspiration and enchantment for many years to come.

*And,* teachers, inspirers, workers of magic and weavers of wonder, thank you all again, from the bottom of my heart, for making this *a goldmine of wisdom.*

*Magic says: 'The world is not at all it appears to be. Every solid object is made of whirling atoms. Everything is in movement - has colour, has sound. Nothing dies. Everything changes. There are Beings, potencies, powers, love infinite and in so many forms you would melt with ecstasy if you could know them all. You can call these Guardian Angels, Extra-Terrestrial Intelligences, Spirits, or whatever you like. Magic knows that you have friends everywhere, that the Universe is conspiring to*

*help you fulfill your dream, that blossoming, flowering and radiating your best is what you were always meant to do - and that life and Spirit and all these Beings around you are ready to help you - at any time.'*
     Philip Carr-Gomm – The Book of English Magic

## Magic:
   *a flickering finger*
   *growing branches.*
   *a tickle turning*
   *numbness into attention.*
   *inner growth*
   *and outer crutch*
   *dancing on the raven's tongue.*
     Enrique Enriquez – Metaphorical Mind Reader

*To the child, wonder and mystery are in everyday things, the things that adults often take for granted! Yet somewhere in the mental maze of our minds lies our child-like innocence. Magic is the yarn that guides us there and when we reach that enchanted place we find that our sadness and worries simply cease to be as important as they were just moments before.*
     Paul Brook – Mentalist

*Think of yourself as a gift to be given. Think only of giving because only in giving can peace and contentment be found. Only through giving can you be aware of the one who gives.*
     Julia Heywood – author of The Barefoot Indian

*If for just one second you can throw off the blindness of material wealth, and see the truly magical wonder of your entire being, including your past lives, then you will no longer suffer from the debilitating, modern-day malady of amnesia of the soul. For one shining moment you would see clearly for the first time.*
     Jenny Smedley – author, O Books

*Something extraordinary happens when we become aware of being alive*
Simon Small – author of From the Bottom of the Pond

*Each of you is a unique creation. There is only one of you with your imagination. Allow the magic of your imagination to bring joy and wonderment into your life everyday.*
Ray Thompson - The Mind Wizard

*see with new eyes*
*into an undiscovered world,*
*flop, flutter, fly into fresh air,*
*see our mother's face,*
*try a note in a new language,*
*dry our feathers;*
*blink in the fierce bright light,*
*learn the iris trick,*
*re-map the forest,*
*soar over the sea,*
*dream the mountain tops.*
Judy Dinnen - Poet

*The Faerie gave humanity music, and when we play in their sacred places, they listen.*
Damh the Bard

*When you communicate with an animal you learn to communicate with yourself. Animals are the true healers. We have much to learn from their capacity to forgive and the depth of the unconditional love they give so freely. A Humpback whale once told me, when describing how to love ourselves, "you all hold the keys to your hearts - you just have to turn the key and let yourself in!*
Madeleine Walker - Animal Communicator and Healer

*When we are lucky to experience the unimaginable mystery, our minds get blown and we want to share this with everyone. There may come a point where we realize that we are actually responsible for the mystery itself because we are truly not separate from it. Then miraculously, it no longer exists as an external dimension but as actual everyday reality!*

Gerard Senehi – The Experimentalist

*It is time in general to get real and do the rich work of spirituality in new contexts and without all the trappings and authorities. We do need guidance and example, but they are not available usually in institutions.*

Thomas Moore – Author of The Re-Enchantment of Everyday Life

*If I were invisible and could whisper into every ear, I would remind each one of their sure beauty, of their great potential to live a joy full life by stretching out with faith to reach their secret dream, standing on toes, eyes bright, arms out-stretched, giving everything. I would remind them that following a heart's dream is the best path, and not listening to that secret voice is to miss out on life's greatest adventure. It surely ain't a dress rehearsal. Seize your own peculiar happiness passionately no matter what and no matter who. There is only Love, and within this world of Atoms of Love we create our stories. So we create glorious ones, golden. What are your most golden dreams? That is what I would whisper.*

Romany – Diva of Magic

*There are unexpected and enchanted moments when I am startled by succinct patterns and patchworks of words that touch the very essence of my being, so delightful they not only gladden and refresh my soul but spark my own creative flame.*

Caroline George - Priest and Mark's 'spiritual sounding board'

*We are a work in progress and should not be too disappointed then when things are not as perfect as we'd like them to be, for all is moving in God's good time, irresistibly towards greater perfection!*

+Alistair Bate - Bishop of The Independent Liberal Catholic Church

*A life without Mystery would be like a heart without LOVE, & where would we be without LOVE?*

Mike Danata – Magician / Singer

*The 'spiritual' and 'shamanic' ritual of the Arts elevates mankind from the realms of passive animalist observer, to that of active Co-Creator.*

June-Elleni Laine – Psychic Artist

*The nature of magic is beauty and death. It is the inevitability of change, the gift of unknowing. I have stood in its flow and yet could not describe it to you. Yet I know magic is one of the few certainties of this world.*

Rob Chapman Rob - Magician/Druid

*God is all about us*
*in the wild skies,*
*the clouds unravelled by the wind,*
*the sun that turns the trees to gold and sea to duck-egg blue,*
*in the gorse that flowers even in the frost,*
*the shades of winter bracken,*
*the lifted wings of swans,*
*the cries of whiffling geese;*
*in the kindness of strangers,*
*in acts of unexpected courtesy,*
*in the fresh companionship of old friends,*
*the love of those whose wedding is near,*
*in the delight of small children'*
*and the quiet courage of the old;*

Trevor Dennis - Author and Vice Dean of Chester Cathedral

*Five minutes from death, before you leave this crumpled earthy joy—*
*what will you look back on with moist sparkly eyes and a smile?*
*You know?*
*Then live it now –*
*to make sure you remember!*
    Simon Parke – Author, Speaker, Retreat Leader


*I am a magician . . . and so are you. We are all magicians—*
*illusionists—who survive, take pleasure, and find meaning in life, by*
*means of the illusions we create. I write to persuade you that such*
*magic runs rampant in our lives and that this is a good thing.*

    *The only way to avoid visual illusion is to keep your eyes closed.*
*The only way to avoid intellectual illusion is to keep your mind closed.*
*The only way to avoid emotional illusion is to keep your heart closed.*
*The only way to avoid spiritual illusion is to live in a closet and hold*
*your nose so you cannot smell the stink of decay. You can do all this*
*successfully, but you pay a price—diminishment.*
    Robert E. Neale – Author / Magician


*To enchant, you must first become enchanted yourself. There is magic*
*in the very word "enchant". We say it, and we feel it. Look at life. Look*
*at nature. Look at the miracles that make up your body and its*
*movement. Consider the amazing power that keeps people living.*
*Consider what the power of the sun does in life, and the influence it has.*
*Open your eyes and look for enchantment. Stop pretending life isn't an*
*unbelievable series of miraculous events. Take off the blinders and see it*
*all for what it really is. I know many of us think if we took off our*
*blinders, we would become disenchanted. It turns out the reverse is*
*true. Open your eyes wide and honestly. Look around fearlessly. Just by*
*taking a walk, magic will happen in front of your very eyes.*
    Kenton Knepper – Wizard Lama


*If you are looking for a miracle, you do not have to journey very far.*
*Deep inside of each of us there is a secret spring welling up continu-*

ously. It's from a divine, hidden source and is the secret of our true humanity. The task, then, is to discover it and let it flow.

Tom Harpur - Author of The Pagan Christ

# Notes

1 The Re-Enchantment of Everyday Life. HarperCollins, New York, 1996. p.ix

2 The Re-Enchantment of Everyday Life. HarperCollins, New York, 1996, p. xiv,xv

3 I wrote this poem after watching the Disney cartoon Pocahontas

4 Anglicanism is a branch of Christianity which sees itself as both standing broadly within the Catholic tradition as well as being Reformed / Protestant

5 Deacon is the first order of the three-fold ministry within the traditional church. Nowadays it is used primarily as an 'apprenticeship' type role

6 Team Vicar refers to a priest who has limited-responsibility for a church, or group of churches within a large team. Ultimate responsibility lies with the Team Rector

7 The Beautiful Life. Bloomsbury, London, 2007, p. 60

8 Pentecostals base their brand of Christianity on the Day of Pentecost, when the Holy Spirit was said to have been poured out on the Church causing all sorts of strange phenomena to occur. Thus they remain a 'Spirit' and 'Miracle' centered tradition

9 Taken from The Magicians Tale. O Books, 2008

10 Everything Belongs. Crossroads, New York, 1999, p. 76

11 An Icon is a beautifully and prayerfully painted depiction of God, Jesus or one of the Saints. They are usually associated with the great Orthodox Churches of the East

12 A Canon is a member of the team clergy who serve a Cathedral

13 Ecclesiological refers to the 'study of the institution of the Church, its orders of ministry, its faith and its practise'

14 My first marriage did not last, but left me with two

wonderful children who are a constant source of pride and joy

15  The Eucharist is the ritual whereby Christians eat and drink bread and wine in memory of the sacrificial death of Jesus. It is called by many names - The Mass, The Holy Communion, The Lord's Supper etc.

16  A Thurible is an incense censer on a chain with / or without bells. It is swung in front of the altar, the bibles, the priests and the congregation as a symbol of holiness and prayer

17  The Magic Mirror. Hermetic Press, Seattle, 2002, p.22

18  Quoted, with permission, from the Leominster Journal

19  Jung for Beginners, Maggie Hyde and Michael McGuiness, Icon, Cambridge 1992, p.6

20  A Stipendiary Minister is a clergyperson who is paid by the Church as opposed to a Non Stipendiary Minister who is voluntary

21  Occasional Offices refer to the services clergy offer the community like Baptisms, Weddings and Funerals

22  Magic and Meaning. Hermetic Press, Seattle, 1995, p. 22

23  Paranormal Magazine. Woking, Surrey, Issue 23

24  The Beautiful Life. Bloomsbury, London, 2007, p. 81

25  The Beautiful Life. Bloomsbury, London, 2007, p. 16

26  Instalment is the ceremony where a new priest is licensed to his or her new parish

27  A Mantra is a repeated word or phrase used in Eastern forms of meditation to still the mind

28  Gathered and edited by Philip Carr-Gomm, of the Order of Bards, Ovates and Druids

29  Paganism is an umbrella term that loosely refers to the multitude of nature based religions and traditions, many of which are literally thousands of years old, others of which are more modern yet are based on ancient understandings of the earth, deity and the spirituality of all life

30  A Grove is the Druid term for what is essentially a spiritual

community like a church. Unlike most churches, however, Groves tend not to have any fixed meeting place. The temple or sacred space is formed by the gathering itself, whenever and wherever it meets, which is often in the open air

31  From the OBOD website. www.Druidry.org

32  Richard Nelson, Nature writer and cultural anthropologist. Quote taken from an internet collection of nature based quotations

33  The Sacraments are the two – Anglican, or seven – Roman Catholic, symbolic 'rituals of grace'. i.e Baptism and Holy Communion

34  The Doctrine of The Atonement refers to the question of how Jesus' death and resurrection makes peace between God and humankind

35  Heather Blakey is an inspirational writer who runs the large internet writing community www.dailywriting.net

36  Winford Manor is now a top notch, and superb value airport hotel closely based near Bristol Airport

37  The Twelve Steps is the Programme of the Alcoholic Anonymous Movement, that helps people recover from alcoholism. It is now applied not just to alcoholism but to many different kinds of addiction, from drugs to excessive shopping.

38  The Gospel of Falling Down. O Books, 2007, ps.81-86

39  Taken from The Wizard's Gift. O Books, 2008, p. 158,159

40  Living Druidry, Piatkus, London 2004, p16

41  The Enneagram is an amazing tool for self discovery and personal transformation. Its roots are at least 2,000 years old, but it has been adapted for use within all sorts of modern day situations – from the business world to religion and spirituality. A quick Google search will get you more than enough links to keep you fascinated for hours

42  In my book, The Wizard's Gift, the main character, Sam, was going to end his life in the forest where I sit and reflect

43  Medicine Cards, David Carson and Jamie Sams, St. Martins Press ©1988-2008 and NATT LLC

44  Magic and Meaning. Hermetic Press, Seattle, 1995. p.35

45  Magic and Meaning. Hermetic Press, Seattle, 1995. p.35

46  In fact theories about the left-right brain dichotomy are now being heavily challenged by certain areas of neuroscience. Even so, they still serve as a useful tool for discussions about the intuitive vs. analytical sides of the human mind

47  Cold Reading is the technique whereby a mentalist, fortune teller or quasi-psychic is able to convince a person that he or she knows far more about them than they actually do.

48  The Re-Enchantment of Everyday Life. HarperCollins, New York, 1996. p.xv

49  Philip Carr-Gomm, Druid Mysteries, Rider, London, 2002, p.164

50  The Druid Animal Oracle, Connections Publishing, London 1996, p.69

51  Fr. Richard Rohr Everything belongs, Crossroads, New York, 1999, ps.111, 112

52  Keeping God Company, SPCK, London 2002, p.67

53  Living Druidry, Piatkus, London 2004, p16

54  The Elements of the Druid Tradition, Element Books, 1996

55  The Elements of the Druid Tradition, Element Books, 1996

56  The Beautiful Life, Bloomsbury, London, 2007, p. 183

57  Keeping God Company, SPCK, London 2002, ps.67, 68

58  Taken, with permission, from Tom Harpur's official website – www.tomharpur.com

59  Taken, with permission, from Tom Harpur's official website – www.tomharpur.com

60  Taken, with permission, from the Celie De website - www.CeileDe.co.uk

61  Brigid's Eye - also known as God's Eyes. It is a cross made of 2 sticks and then wool, or rags or threads bound round the cross to form a diamond shape. They can then be hung in

windows or trees as a symbol of protection

62  There are eight commonly celebrated festivals of the modern pagan movement. They are related to the seasons and to the solar equinoxes and solstices. They are celebrated in different ways by the different groups.

63  Samhain is pronounced Sow-en. It marks the beginning of the Pagan year, occurring around the end of October / beginning of November. It is often seen as a festival of celebration of the dead, and is referred to, by non-pagans, as Halloween and by Christians as All Souls Day

64  Yule, or Winter Solstice is the festival of celebration of the re-birth of the sun. It is the period where the sun reaches it south-most point, and the days begin to lengthen again. It is no co-incidence that many 'sun-god-myths' centre around a god-man-figure who is said to have been born at this time of year. Christ's birth, on the 25th of December, is just one of many Winter Solstice god-man heroes

65  The festival of Imbolc occurs at the very beginning of February, and is traditionally regarded as the first day of Spring

66  For more information on The Ceile De go to www.CeileDe.com

67  Extract taken from Principles of Druidry, Thorsons, 1998

68  Excerpt taken from *What do Druids Believe?* Philip Carr-Gomm, Granta. 2006

69  The Rt Revd Alistair Bate M.A.Div, Liberal Catholic Apostolic Church, Edinburgh, 2008. For more information on Bishop Alistair's Christian-Druid Grove please see www.geocities.com/b.bishopalistair/Christian_Druid_Order.html

70  Living Drudiry, Piatkus, London 2004, p. 6,7

71  Alban Elfed is The Feast of the Autumn Equinox. The Light of the Sun in the Wheel of the Year stands in the West, in the Place of balance between the Light and the Darkness. This is

a time of the Great Tides, the Gateway of the Year

72 A Seedgroup is a simple, small fellowship group made up of OBOD members

73 Cernunnos and Rhiannon are Celtic god/goddesses. As 'Lord of the other world,' Cernunnos was the Celtic horned god, the stag, the lord of the animals and the world of nature. Originally he was lord of the hunt and is associated with prosperity and abundance, good fortune and virility. Rhiannon is the beautiful horse goddess

74 M. Oldfield Howey 1923: The Horse in Magic and Myth, Dover Publications, Mineola, N.Y. 2002, p.43

# BOOKS

O is a symbol of the world, of oneness and unity. In different cultures it also means the "eye," symbolizing knowledge and insight. We aim to publish books that are accessible, constructive and that challenge accepted opinion, both that of academia and the "moral majority."

Our books are available in all good English language bookstores worldwide. If you don't see the book on the shelves ask the bookstore to order it for you, quoting the ISBN number and title. Alternatively you can order online (all major online retail sites carry our titles) or contact the distributor in the relevant country, listed on the copyright page.

See our website www.o-books.net for a full list of over 500 titles, growing by 100 a year.

And tune in to myspiritradio.com for our book review radio show, hosted by June-Elleni Laine, where you can listen to the authors discussing their books.

MySpiritRadio